HELP!
*For Parents of
School-Age Children
and Teenagers*

HELP!

For Parents of School-Age Children and Teenagers

Jean Illsley Clarke
and Deane Gradous, Sara Monser, Gail Nordeman,
Harold Nordeman, Sandra Sittko, and Christine
Ternand, M.D.

HarperSanFrancisco
A Division of HarperCollinsPublishers

FIRST REVISED EDITION

Library of Congress Cataloging-in-Publication Data
Clarke, Jean Illsley.
    Help! for parents of school-age children and teenagers / Jean Illsley Clarke . . . [et al.] —1st rev. ed.
        p.   cm.
    Rev. ed. of: Help! for parents of children from ages six to twelve years and Help! for parents of teenagers.
    Includes bibliographical references and index.
    ISBN: 0–06–250204–2
    1. Child rearing—United States.   2. Teenagers—United States. I. Help! for parents of children from ages six to twelve years.   II. Help! for parents of teenagers.   III. Title.
HQ769.C613   1993
649'.1—dc20   92–56402
                                                                                                    CIP

93 94 95 96 97 ❖ RRD-H 10 9 8 7 6 5 4 3 2 1

This edition is printed on acid-free paper that meets the American National Standards Institute Z39.48 Standard.

To the hundreds of wise and thoughtful parents
who in this book have shared
some of what they have learned
so that other parents may know
that they are not alone,
that they have choices, and
that they need not reinvent the wheel.

Contents

Appreciations

We offer our appreciation to:

- The many parents and foster parents who shared their wisdom in our Suggestion Circles, for without them this book would not exist

- All the facilitators of the parenting class, Self-Esteem: A Family Affair, who contributed to this book

- The clients at A Growing Place, Cincinnati, Ohio, and Healdsburg, California, for their questions and suggestions

- Joanne Smith, Glenn Smith, Roxanne Michelson, Sandee Goldsmith, Sheri Goldsmith, Ron Kubes, Kay Kubes, Mary Kay Truitt, Susan K. Keane, Rosemarie Zawacki, and Margaret Matsko for their special efforts.

We especially thank:

- Our many colleagues in transactional analysis for their knowledge and insights

- Peter Geittmann and Judy Scanga for their support

- Paul Singh and the pediatricians at the Saint Paul Group Health Medical Center for their support

- Bobbi Mlekodaj for her help at the initiation of this book

- Lois White, Lillian Weger, Maggie Lawrence, Connie Dawson, Mary Paananen, Lonnie Bell, and Carole Gesme for their careful reading of the manuscript and for their many helpful suggestions

- Deane Gradous for conceiving the idea of publishing in book form the lists of questions and responses compiled through Suggestion Circles

- Dr. Christine Ternand for sharing her medical perspective in writing about abuse and for reading the suggestions for medical accuracy

- Becky Monson, Athalie Terry, and Barbara Beystrom for their support, encouragement, and dedicated typing

- Tom Grady for his helpful editing and continuous encouragement

- All those with whom we have studied, worked, and learned

- Our parents, siblings, spouses, and children for teaching us about the importance of families.

The Editors

Foreword

This book offers double help, since it is really two books in one: *Help! For Parents of School-Age Children* and *Help! For Parents of Teenagers*.

The first section makes clear what parents have always known—that parenting the six- to twelve-year-old child is not the uneventful, tranquil experience some developmental theorists have led us to expect. Like every developmental stage, the period from six to twelve years is dynamic, challenging, joyous, and sometimes stormy and difficult. Yet despite its difficulties, many parents especially cherish this stage of their children's development. It is a time when children grow and learn at dizzying speeds and a time when parents can and must have a tremendous influence on the direction of this development. Much to our delight as parents, children at this age are likely to seek out and openly welcome our help and guidance.

For families, this developmental period is a time to enjoy doing things together—playing, talking, working, creating, and exploring. It is a time to help children prepare for the reality and responsibilities of adolescence and adulthood, a time to promote open discussion and provide clear guidance about many family values and traditions, a time to talk about such issues as sex, drugs, alcohol, and destructive behavior. *The foundation for future communication on these and other vital issues is built stone by stone during these years.*

The second section of the book is for parents of adolescents. The teenage years are at once magical and disquieting for both teenagers and their parents. Erik Erikson tells us that the major growth task facing teens is the development of a sense of personal identity. This identity, or sense of self, must be strong and healthy so that teenagers can handle successfully their emerging responsibilities as nurturing and contributing adults. A major task of our own middle-age years is to assist teenage children in becoming responsible and happy adults.

The delight of the teen years includes the many opportunities that parents and teenagers have to develop a new, more adult-to-adult relationship. The challenge is to learn how to pace the unfolding of this relationship. We know that teenagers continue to *need* parental guidance. We know that they also *want* counsel and support, although they may be reluctant to admit such desires even to themselves.

The child and parent issues that are addressed by the questions and suggestions in this book are likely to be scattered along the path from childhood to adulthood. Each issue can be either an obstacle or an opportunity for both parents and their children. If they miss this mutual learning and teaching opportunity, both parents and their offspring will be cheated.

This is a book for, by, and about parents. It is a testament to the compassion, understanding, and wisdom that parents have to offer each other. Most of the familiar problems that face school-age children, teens, and their parents are discussed here. A glance at the table of contents might raise parents' anxieties about the potential difficulties they face, but the wealth of suggestions offered in each section of this book should serve to reduce these anxieties. For each problem, readers encounter a range of sensible options. These suggestions are not only wise in themselves but they also encourage readers to combine, adapt, and invent ways of coping that will best fit the specific situation that parents face.

This book, as its editors caution and as its title suggests, is not about the times when things are going smoothly. It is, nevertheless, an optimistic book. Parents will find comfort in the suggestions, which are simple, upbeat, clear, and practical. The writing is warm and friendly, and readers will feel cared for and empowered, not intimidated or demeaned. This approach should help parents, their children, and teenagers learn to cope wisely and effectively with the stresses that they will inevitably face.

Dorothea Cudaback, D.S.W.
Human Relations Specialist,
University of California Cooperative Extension

What Is This Book About?

This is a book written for parents by parents.

It is a book for the days when you don't know what to do or for those when what you're doing isn't working. It is *not* a theoretical book about the times when things are going smoothly. It *is* a book of specific, practical suggestions on how to handle problems for which parents have sought help in parenting classes around the country.

These parents have participated in groups led by a facilitator who is trained in the techniques used in Self-Esteem: A Family Affair classes. One of these techniques, called the Suggestion Circle, is used to collect options for parents with problems or questions. Here's how it works. In class, members sit in a circle and listen to a parent describe a problem. Each member of the circle then offers his or her best suggestion for dealing with it. In this way, the person with the problem benefits from the collective wisdom and experience of the whole group and goes home with a list of suggestions or options.

The Suggestion Circle process is different from brainstorming, which encourages people to offer every idea that comes to mind. It is also different from listening to the teacher or the expert provide the "correct answer." In a Suggestion Circle, *every* answer comes from an "authority"—a parent, foster parent, uncle, aunt, or grandparent. And every answer is "correct," since it worked for the person who discovered it—sometimes after many years of experience. The resulting list provides a variety of suggestions and encourages flexibility in the listener or reader. It may suggest a new way of perceiving the problem. You decide what might work for you.

We chose the questions in this book from these Suggestion Circles because they represent problems that we hear about repeatedly in classes or that seem particularly difficult for parents. Leaders collected the suggestions and asked the parents if we could share their responses with you in this book. Each question, with its related responses, includes the name of the first facilitator or group who sent the problem to us and the location of that class or group. Since similar problems come up in different parts of the country, we have combined suggestions from more than one group.

You will notice that often the answers contradict one another. This needn't bother you. Parents, children, and homes differ, and what works for one may not work for another or at another time. *Use what works for you!*

You will find the questions grouped in clusters according to subject matter. We have eliminated any ideas that advocated violence, both because child abuse is illegal and because we do not believe that violence helps children. We have also eliminated suggestions that implied that parents or children are helpless or that a problem was not serious. We assume that if parents ask for help, the problems are important and serious to them.

We have also outlined briefly the characteristic tasks of the stages of development covered in this book, and we have described how parents may abuse school-age children and teens if they misunderstand those tasks. We have given short explanations of affirmations, recycling, and other topics that are important parts of the Self-Esteem: A Family Affair class and that are referred to throughout the book.

So here they are, some short reference pieces and 178 collections of the best ideas on parenting, from parents who have been there, to you who are there now.

The Editors

How to Use This Book

You can use this book to help you think. When you want ideas about how to solve a problem, look in the table of contents for a chapter title that seems to include your problem. For example, for the problem of children arguing with each other, look under "Brothers and Sisters, Friends and Peers." Or look in the index for words that describe your problem (like *arguing, name-calling, sibling rivalry,* or *competition*), and then read about the problems that sound most like yours.

Reading about what other parents have done will remind you that there are many ways to solve problems and that you can discover and try out new ways that work for you and your child. If you read a list over several times, you will probably find ideas that you missed the first time. Some of the suggestions may not fit your situation or your parenting style, and some of the lists contain contradictions, since there are lots of ways to raise children. Think about which suggestions sound useful for your particular problem.

Our purpose is *not* to give "one right answer" but to support and stimulate your thinking by offering the wisdom of hundreds of the real child-rearing experts—parents themselves.

Remember that these suggestions are not listed in order of importance. They were offered by a circle of people. If we had printed them in circles, this would have been a very big book indeed! We have printed them in lists in order to make this book convenient to use, not to imply that the top suggestion is best.

Use the short sections at the beginning and ending of each part of the book as you need them. For a picture of normal behavior for children at a particular developmental stage, read "Ages and Stages" and "Common Pitfalls." You can use this information to think about whether your expectations are reasonable.

The "Affirmations for Growth" sections are about healthy messages or beliefs that children at each stage need to decide are true for them. Look at "Structuring for Success" and "Structuring for Responsibility and Independence" for ways to foster responsibility in children. The section called "Parents Get Another Chance—Recycling" reminds us that our own growth never stops and that we, too, have developmental tasks to accomplish.

The appendixes contain more helpful information. If you are distressed about how anger is expressed inappropriately or repressed in your household, consider using a "fuss box." There are also directions to follow for when you want to run your own Suggestion Circle and ideas about where to go for additional support.

So read and think. Honor yourself for the many things you do well with your children. Celebrate your growth and the growth of your children. Change when you need to. Remember that your parents did the best they could and that you are doing the best you can. If you want to learn some new ways of parenting, it is never too late to start.

Note: Throughout this book, we have alternated masculine and feminine pronouns; in one set of suggestions, the child will be a "she," in the next a "he." In each case, please read "all children."

—*Jean Illsley Clarke*

Structuring for Success

In your role as a loving parent, you help your children by structuring for their success and by teaching them how to structure for their own success. What does this mean? Structuring for success is the process of creating and applying systems of rules, customs, rewards, values, procedures, and expectations that help everyone, including children, to live successful lives inside and outside the family.

How do parents structure for success? Through insight and effort, parents set up working and learning situations in which children find it easier to succeed than to fail. Parents set firm boundaries, encourage and reward ethical behavior, and cherish family traditions. They reward desired behaviors, make and enforce rules, and teach lifetime skills. Parents provide support to children in their most important tasks: learning to relate with others and going to school.

How do children learn to structure for their own success? They learn by experiencing the positive and negative consequences of their actions. They learn by observing how their parents and other adults live successful lives. For an example, let's look at how children structure for success in managing money.

- They do it at age six by having a small amount of money of their own to spend or save as they wish.

- They do it at age ten by deciding with parental guidance whether and how to budget for a special purchase.

- They do it at age twelve by earning extra money through their own hard work.
- They do it at all ages by observing how their parents and others make decisions that involve earning, saving, investing, and spending money.

Families structure for success in all lifetime skills in much the same way—in small steps.

Why are learning and using lifetime skills so important? Just as we feel good about learning successful new ways to parent, so do our children feel good when they learn new ways to do well at school, to acquire new friends, or to care for their pets. We parents contribute greatly to our children's success in school and in society when we set up a home environment that encourages children to finish their homework before they watch television and to participate in the family chores so that the whole family can go to the library or to the circus.

In the questions and answers that follow, parents often suggest providing structure in the form of rules, rewards, traditions, and so on. Our school-age children's success at least partially hangs on the loving attention and the hard work that go into providing the needed structure. "How to Make and Enforce Rules" in Part One talks further about this issue.

Deane Gradous

Parents Get Another Chance— Recycling

The sections entitled "Parents Get Another Chance— Recycling" at the beginning of each part offer specific ideas about tasks that parents can recycle when their children are in the related developmental stage.

When children are increasing their skills and challenging the rules, parents sometimes begin to chafe at the rules in their own lives and decide to learn new skills, too. One of the benefits of caring for six- to twelve-year-old children, for example, is that parents can use this time to rework or recycle their own internal values and structures and the how and why of the things they do.

Often, parents of adolescents find the teenage years easier than the earlier stages because their children can be reasoned with and are becoming more and more responsible. Other parents, however, are distressed by teenagers' behaviors, interests, values, resistances, and mercurial mood swings.

What Is Recycling?

Recycling is the name given to the rhythmic, cyclical growth process through which individuals learn, often without noticing it, how to accomplish important developmental tasks in ever more competent and sophisticated ways. Pamela Levin discusses the theory of recycling in *Becoming the Way We Are*. Recycling does not mean that we adults regress to a childlike state but rather that our life experiences demand that we continually develop more skillful ways of completing old life-supporting tasks at the same time that we are working on new adult-stage tasks. Besides having a natural rhythm for the development of these adult tasks, we parents are often triggered to recycle whatever stages our children are in. I have talked with hundreds of parents about this idea. Many of them have reported, often with some surprise, that they *are* working on some of the same tasks as their children. This is a normal, healthy, and hopeful aspect of living with growing children.

Some parents of adolescents relish the unfolding of the emerging adult and enjoy the "letting go," but others resist the separation and try to maintain control. Almost all parents find the daily demands of nurturing, challenging, and setting limits for adolescents taxing at times. Whatever parents feel when children go through the transition from childhood to adulthood, one of the benefits of this period is that it triggers parents to recycle or to continue working on their own tasks of becoming whole, separate human beings, of owning their sexuality, and of expanding their concept of their place in the larger world. Reexamining our needs for nurturing, exploring, and deciding who we are and what rules we live by can parallel these stages in our adolescents. Parents who "recycle" and create better ways to do old tasks along with their kids may make the journey through the teen years a more satisfying adventure.

Jean Illsley Clarke

HELP!
*For Parents of
School-Age Children
and Teenagers*

I

Help!
For Parents of School-Age Children

Ages and Stages

The job of six- to twelve-year-old children is to learn many new skills and how to do them well in their own way. To achieve these tasks, they practice skills and explore rules. They consider what rules are, how they are made, and how they can be broken. In addition, children think about what values and morals are and how their values and morals contribute to who they are. This exploration of rules and values enables them to learn how to take care of themselves and how to guide their lives.

How do they do this?

- *They ask questions.* The information they gather helps them to do things in their own way.

- *They practice.* They engage in a wide variety of activities, and they willingly practice over and over the skills in which they're interested.

- *They compare.* They may say, "At Sally's house they do it this way." "At Tommy's house they get to stay up until ten. Why can't I?" "Ann has designer jeans. When do I get mine?"

- *They test.* They test their parents' rules to the *n*th degree. They need to determine which rules are firm and which can be broken.

- *They disagree.* They need to know that they can disagree and still be loved. Disagreeing helps them form their own opinions. Learning to disagree in a safe and accepting setting will enable them to be assertive and not to yield to peer pressure. A healthy argument or debate shows them that children and adults are entitled to their own opinions, thoughts, and feelings. Parents' willingness to engage in a healthy argument or debate reinforces the belief that children are entitled to their own opinions.

- *They recycle earlier developmental tasks.*

The job of the parent is

- To give unconditional love

- To expose children to a wide variety of opportunities

- To give accurate information

- To give children the chance to explore different skills

- To teach parental values and to encourage children to internalize values that respect self, others, and the environment

- To maintain the necessary structure for success, including making and enforcing rules consistently

- To expect the six- to twelve-year-old to challenge those rules. The parent must be prepared to explain, defend, and examine the rules he or she has set. The parent must decide which rules are negotiable and which are not negotiable.

To enable the child to test rules, the parents must create a protective and nurturing environment. They respect the child and listen to the child's story, problem, or opinion. They expect him to think and to separate fantasy from reality. The parents explain their values to the child. Explanations of skills, rules, and values help children understand why rules are needed. The child also needs affirmations that he is expected to think clearly, to solve problems, and to argue. Some children who are busy learning and exploring rules are warm, open, and affectionate. Others seem quite self-contained, while others are downright cantankerous.

This explaining, defending, and challenging of rules may tax the energy of the most enthusiastic parent. In order to maintain enthusiasm and powerful parenting skills, parents must take good care of themselves. They must be sure that they are getting their own needs met and that they are modeling lives filled with supportive structures and functional rules. Thus, parenting a six- to twelve-year-old gives parents the opportunity to examine their own rules for living and to change the rules that do not work.

Sandra Sittko and Deane Gradous

Affirmations for Growth—
Structure

At each period or stage of growth in children's lives, there are certain tasks they need to master and certain decisions they need to make if they are to grow into loving, capable, responsible adults.

Parents can help children master these tasks by providing safe, structured, stimulating environments and experiences. Parents can encourage their children to make appropriate decisions by challenging inappropriate behavior and by giving their children affirmations.

What are affirmations? Affirmations are all the things we do or say that imply that children are lovable and capable. We affirm children with our words and our actions, our body language, our facial expressions, and our tone of voice.

Here are some special affirming messages that will help children in this stage of growth (ages six through twelve), as they develop their own structures, competence, and values and learn about the relevance of rules.

Affirmations for Structure

- You can think before you say yes or no and learn from your mistakes.

- You can trust your intuition to help you decide what to do.

- You can find a way of doing things that works for you.

- You can learn the rules that help you live with others.

- You can learn when and how to disagree.

- You can think for yourself and get help instead of staying in distress.

- I love you even when we differ; I love growing with you.

You *give* these affirmations by the way you interact with your children, challenge their thinking, and encourage them to test values, examine rules, acquire information and skills, and experience consequences.

In addition to all the things you do, you can *say* these affirmations directly in supportive, loving ways.

Belief in these affirmations helps children achieve independence and encourages them to develop responsible behavior. The affirmations are powerful antidotes to peer pressure. Giving them may take effort, especially on days when the children are hassling you and pushing the limits to find out which rules are firm and important and what happens when rules are broken.

Of course, you have to believe these messages yourself or they become confusing or crazy double messages. If you don't understand or believe an affirmation, don't give that one until you do believe it.

Once human beings have entered each developmental stage, they need to receive the affirmations for that stage for the rest of their lives, so children continue to need the affirmations from earlier stages. Those messages support their being, their exploring and doing, their thinking, and their identity. These affirmations are listed in "Developmental Affirmations for All Ages" at the back of this book.

The Being affirmations reinforce our right to exist and have needs, to be loved and cared for.

The Exploring and Doing messages focus on the need to reach out and to explore, to initiate, and to be creative.

The Thinking messages support separation and independence.

The messages for Identity focus on independence, self-image, and power to support independent thinking.

If you believe, from observing your child's attitude or behavior, that your child did not "get" some of these affirmations during her younger years, focus on those affirmations now. Remember, it is never too late for you to start believing and offering the affirmations.

You can read more about what affirmations mean and don't mean and how to use them in families in Clarke's *Self-Esteem: A Family Affair* and Clarke and Dawson's *Growing Up Again*. (See "Resources.")

When you discover additional affirmations that your child needs, write them down and give them to your child.

Jean Illsley Clarke

Structure
—Ages six through twelve and ever after—

You can think before you say yes or no and learn from your mistakes.

You can trust your intuition to help you decide what to do.

You can find a way of doing things that works for you.

You can learn the rules that help you live with others.

You can learn when and how to disagree.

You can think for yourself and get help instead of staying in distress.

I love you even when we differ; I love growing with you.

**Copy these ovals and color them light blue.
Post them for daily reading.**

Parents of School-Age Children Get Another Chance—Recycling

Recycling the Tasks of Internalizing Our Own Values and Structures

While the children are busy learning new skills and exploring the importance of rules, parents are busy learning, too. They learn new skills to help their children, to support their own career advancement, or to nurture their own growth. Parents who are pushed by children of this age to enforce and defend family rules can take this opportunity to reevaluate these rules, along with any personal rules they have set for themselves, dropping outdated ones, changing and updating others, and strengthening their basic values.

Parents who did not learn the skills of hassling during their own childhood can practice that assertive skill now as they learn to challenge their children to think clearly. Hassling in a nurturing way is one way of connecting with a child who is getting less parental touching than little children get. Hassling involves choosing a topic and bantering about it in a way that does not criticize the child or the parent, and that encourages the child to think about the topic from several points of view. Often it is absurd and amusing. Parents can learn to handle hassling initiated by the child in a good-natured way that keeps it enjoyable for the parent while it challenges the child to think.

The affirmations that are helpful to our children (and that are listed in the previous section) are also healthy for us. Because many of us never received or decided not to believe some of these healthy messages (or we only believed them partly), this is an ideal time to accept these messages for ourselves and to claim more of our ability to be whole, healthy, joyful adults. If you didn't get the affirmations you needed the first time around, you can take them now as you offer them to your children.

(For more information on recycling, see also "Parents Get Another Chance—Recycling" at the beginning of this book.)

Jean Illsley Clarke

Common Pitfalls

Sometimes, as children go about their developmental tasks, they do things that are misinterpreted by adults, who then may be overly severe or hurtful in an attempt to stop or control these normal behaviors. Parents may believe that they are "disciplining," but when they punish their children for doing what is developmentally correct and normal, children are hurt physically or emotionally. In addition, parents who do not understand the importance for their children of developing internal responsibility at this age may overindulge by not insisting on the child's gradual assumption of personal responsibility or by not insisting that the child obey rules.

The following behaviors of children this age are frequently misunderstood:

- School-age children are deciding about their own rules. They question all rules, including those of their parents. Many caring adults misinterpret this as "mouthing off." Parents can be firm on a few important rules and spend time with the kids negotiating others.

- As peers become more important to children, sometimes caring adults may see this as a rejection of the parent. They may then neglect or abandon the child. It is important to remember that children want both parents and friends, even if they don't say so. The adults must be responsible for getting their own companionship needs met and not depend on the child to meet them.

- Children this age show signs of rational, adult thinking.

Adults sometimes seize on this sign of new thinking as an opportunity to push children with a "hurry-and-grow-up-fast" message. It is important to let children be children.

- Children this age need to spend time with their parents. The "quality time" that parents spent with preschoolers is more difficult to schedule during this stage when children's attentions and priorities turn toward their peers. But parents must spend enough time with school-age children for "quality time" to emerge. Sometimes "quality time" is just "hanging out," not being entertained or instructed or programmed. Children need their parents to "be with" them.

- These children need to practice effective ways of getting along with others. Adults who do not expect and demand some level of respectful behavior cheat children of their right to learn positive ways to interact.

- At this age, children are frequently encountering social systems outside the family, such as school, Little League, and so on. When a child has a problem in one of these organizations, the parents may inadvertently be so upset about how the behavior reflects on them that they forget to focus on the child and the problem. They may be confused about what the child is responsible for and what the adults are responsible for. Parents need to support their children and help the children problem solve.

- Six- to twelve-year-old children are beginning to develop secondary sexual characteristics. Unfortunately, the media and others in our society often offer the fantasy that these children are highly desirable sexually. *Any sexual touching of children by adults is abuse.*

Christine Ternand, M.D.

Keeping School-Age Children Safe

Since children this age are learning about values and rules, parents need to provide clear structure. Parents who keep their children safe and who do not abuse or neglect their children do the following:

- They remember that children need some clear rules (for example, about bedtime on school nights, chores, and so on) and that children need to have those rules enforced in a caring, consistent manner.

- They make certain their children are capable of staying alone before leaving them alone. They pay special attention to the child's ability to follow safety rules, and they start by leaving the child alone for short periods of time during daylight hours.

- They ensure that children use seat belts on all car trips— whether short or long.

- They give children permission to say no to peer pressure.

- They help children establish a sense of personal responsibility by assigning age-appropriate chores and maintaining a structure for them. This structure allows children to learn how to do the chores and then encourages them to assume responsibility for those jobs on an ongoing basis.

- Parents should become aware of the extent of alcohol abuse and drug abuse in their child's environment and take action to protect the child from that abuse. They should refuse to serve their children alcoholic beverages. The chances of alcohol causing liver damage in a child this age are much greater than in an adult.

- They meet the responsible adults of any home where their child spends significant time. They also meet any adults who will be alone with their child for periods of time (such as people for whom their child baby-sits and adults who lead groups for these children).

- They meet their children's friends.

- They establish clear lines of communication with the parents of their children's friends in order to establish consistent rules about safety.

- They maintain open lines of communication with the school system, and they follow up on problems noted.

- They establish themselves as a reliable source of information about people, the world, and sex. They explain about sexual growth to their children caringly, lovingly, and knowledgeably, or they get a specially trained adult to do it. In addition, they supply the children with accurate printed information about these topics. It is important for children this age to receive lots of nurturing touch, but they should *never* be touched sexually by adults. Children should know that they are to report sexual touches or sexual invitations by adults or teenagers to their parents.

- Parents need to overcome their own fears and confusions about possible unplanned pregnancies and AIDS so that they can give their child accurate and perhaps life-saving information.

- Finally, they reevaluate their own value system and use common, daily opportunities to affirm those values to their child.

If you suspect abuse of any kind, find a way to protect your child. Get help if you need it. Report the abuser to the child protection service in your area. See "Where to Go for Additional Support."

Christine Ternand, M.D.

How to Make and Enforce Rules

Parents have conflicting feelings about rules. Am I too strict? Am I being too lenient? Are these the right rules for our family? The following steps for making and enforcing rules can be used as a guide:

1. **Think about what and who the rules are for.**

   For example:

   - Some rules protect the child's health and social welfare.
   - Some rules help the family function smoothly.
   - Some rules help children relate positively to the outside world.
   - Some rules protect the whole society or the environment.

2. **Consider your personal and family values.**

   For example:

   - Healthy bodies are important. Families need rules about sleep, exercise, and nutrition.
   - Rules about respectful language and about personal property lead to a peaceful family life.

3. **Set specific, reasonable, observable, enforceable rules.**

   For example:

   - Every day each family member eats something from each level of the Food Guide Pyramid.

4. Decide if rules are negotiable or nonnegotiable.

Nonnegotiable rules teach children to comply. They focus on such issues as safety, health, legality, religious observance, parental preference, and community custom.

For example:

- Every day each family member eats something from each level of the Food Guide Pyramid.

Negotiable rules teach children to think and to assume responsibility. They must be appropriate to the child's skill and maturity level. They focus on such issues as money, grades, family convenience, chores, social manners, clothing, and sports.

For example:

- A six-year-old may negotiate about when during the day to eat some fruit. A twelve-year-old may negotiate about whether to make or to buy pizza for a gathering of friends, who will pay for it, and whether to ask friends to bring some of the food.

5. Establish clear expectations that help children learn to consider who, what, when, where, how long, how much, how often, and why.

For example:

- Negotiations about the food part of a party with friends might result in the following decisions: Parents will supply ingredients for pizzas, fruit, milk, and soda pop. Children will make pizzas and may make cookies the day before. The children will pay for potato chips.

6. Move from negotiating a few rules with a six-year-old to negotiating many rules with a twelve-year-old.

7. Set rewards for compliance.

Notice and reward children when they obey the rules.
For example:

- For choosing and eating a balanced diet, children can move from getting gold stars daily at age six, to getting gifts occasionally at age nine, to internalizing the enjoyment of a healthy body at age twelve.

8. Set consequences for noncompliance.

Rely on natural consequences when doing so will not harm the child and will cause discomfort soon enough to reinforce the desired behavior. Use logical consequences when natural ones don't fit.

For example:

- Natural consequence: Overeating of junk food causes a stomachache.

- Logical consequence: Overconsumption of junk food means no snacks except fruit for two weeks.

9. Enforce rules consistently.

If you have difficulty enforcing rules, examine your own rules about rules. Rules about rules include: "Rules are made to be broken." "Rules must always be followed." "Break rules; just don't get caught." "Rules are made to help people live together."

- Do your rules about rules support consistent enforcement?

10. Consider changing your rules.

- If it's necessary for your children's welfare, change your own rules about rules. Compare your rules with those of other adults who care for your children. Do what you need to do in order to reach an agreement about rules with those other adults.

The Editors

Coaching: An Essential Skill

Coaching is a respectful, growth-oriented interaction between parent and child about something of value.

There are two types of coaching:

1) Building skilled behavior

2) Correcting unskilled or ineffective behavior.

Successful coaches are able to:

1) Observe and describe current behaviors and their results

2) Describe or demonstrate desired behaviors and their expected results

3) Encourage skill building.

Typically, coaching is most needed when the child can perform a task at some level but lacks the motivation or the skills to perform at the desired level. Coaches provide direction and support. They also help to build confidence and enthusiasm. As they coach, they hold the child responsible for learning and performing the new behavior.

Listening, observing, proposing, encouraging, insisting, challenging, and approving are some basic skills of a coach. Raging, yelling, name-calling, and being exasperated are not useful coaching skills. Skilled coaches know that their own emotional reactions will not change a child's past behavior. What does matter to them is the child's behavior in the future. Future-focused coaching is respectful, change-oriented, and disciplined. Successful coaching:

Is respectful of the child

Is focused on the difference between what is and what is desired to be

Avoids causing children to worry about or despair of their shortcomings

Provides for positive, comfortable interactions that inspire confidence in the learner

Proceeds through a disciplined, structured process.

Steps in Coaching for Skills

1. Set clear objectives.

   For example: Child will learn to bake muffins.

2. Divide the task into manageable units.

   a. Find recipe.

   b. Turn on oven to correct temperature.

   c. Collect and measure ingredients.

   d. Combine ingredients.

   e. Prepare baking pans.

   f. Set timer or watch the clock.

   g. Put away ingredients.

   h. Cool muffins before turning out of pan.

   i. Wash and put away pan, clean sink and counter.

3. Choose with the child what steps you will demonstrate, what steps you will do together, and what steps the child will do while you observe. Gradually during repeated baking sessions the child will learn to complete the task independently, asking for help only when time is short or when he wants companionship.

4. Give positive feedback for each step accomplished and a few suggestions for improvement. Describe the desired outcome.

   "I see you already know how to grease the muffin tins."
   "Next time, if you don't stir the mix so much, the muffins won't have tunnels."
   "These muffins are good—brown on top and light and fluffy. They are a little dark on the bottom, but they taste good, and the kitchen looks great, too. What baking time will you write on the recipe so they'll be done just right next time?"

5. Celebrate finishing.

   Enjoy eating the muffins together.
   Save a muffin for someone special.
   Report the achievement to someone special.

6. Plan for or anticipate the next skill-building session.

   "Will you help me make muffins for Easter breakfast?"

After a successful coaching experience, both you and your child will feel positive about each other. You will earn the privileges of closeness and trust over and over again through successful coaching.

Deane Gradous and Jean Illsley Clarke

Chapter 1

Rules, Responsibilities, and Money

1. I plan to limit my children's TV watching. Can someone help me make the rules so it will be easier for me and my children to stick to them?

- Set up a system. Have a reward for keeping to the new schedule that you set together.

- Spell out which programs are acceptable, and ask your children to pick a certain number from within that group.

- Hold a family meeting. Discuss everyone's wants and needs, and then set family TV rules. Read Dreikurs, Gould, and Corsini's *Family Council*. (See "Resources.")

- Together, select programs to watch for the week, and circle them in the TV schedule.

- Give each child a certain number of quarters for the week. Have the child pay for each program watched. If all the money isn't used by the end of the week, the child may spend it as she wishes. Or you can use marbles instead of money.

- Set a family rule that all schoolwork or homework must be completed before the TV can be watched, and hold everybody to it.

- On Sunday morning with the family, identify the informational and entertainment shows allowed for the week. Limit TV watching to those.

- Together, decide ahead of time how conflicts over who picks the show will be resolved.

- Post the rules on the refrigerator door.

Thanks to Christine Ternand,
Suggestion Circle from Saint Paul, Minnesota

2. How can I know how much housework to expect of my child?

- Check out his age and ability (can he do the task, or can he learn how?) when determining what tasks to assign.

- Start by expecting him to take care of his own possessions and room. Give him small household chores, and reward him for their completion. Say, "We all share in the family work. Thank you."

- Hold a family council so that the family can decide together how much will be expected of each member. See Dreikurs, Gould, and Corsini's *Family Council.* (See "Resources.")

- Have a job list. The child can choose several small jobs or one big job from the list.

- Certainly kids six and over should handle the daily care of their own rooms and help with total household care. Ten-year-olds can do almost any chore (but slavery is illegal).

- Assign tasks according to age and ability, and stick to the expectation that the tasks will be done. Children will need this ability to finish things later in life when they do things on their own.

(See also questions 5, 8, 24, and 26.)

Thanks to Barbara Morgan,
Suggestion Circle from Seattle, Washington

3. I have a twelve-year-old daughter who is behaving irresponsibly. How can I help her be more responsible?

- Show her how to do things, and expect her to do them well.

- Remind her often that you love her, and tell her when you notice her doing something well.

- When you are angry about something she hasn't done, tell her, and then insist that she do it.

- Be clear about your expectations.

- When she thinks clearly, compliment her thinking.

- Remember, what you stroke is what you get. If she only gets attention when she messes up, she will probably continue to mess up.

- Sit down with her, and the two of you write up a list of rules to which you both agree. Decide together on rewards when she keeps the rules and consequences when she breaks them.

- Let her experience the logical consequences of her behavior—for example, replace her lost gloves with a less expensive pair, and have her pay for the new pair.

- Make sure she knows what you consider irresponsible behavior and what its results are.

- The Eyres' book, *Teaching Children Responsibility*, describes many different ways of helping children become responsible. (See "Resources.")

(See also questions 10, 17, and "Structuring for Success.")

Thanks to Marilyn Sackariason,
Suggestion Circle from Minneapolis, Minnesota

4. When I start to play a game with my eight-year-old son, he hassles over the rules and generally ruins the fun. What can I do?

- Do some other activity with him instead of playing that game.

- When he *is* fun to be with, tell him so.

- Turn the hassling into fun, enjoy it, and learn how to hassle playfully yourself.

- Stop playing when it becomes unpleasant.

- Ask him if he wants an arbitrator to decide on the rules.

- Hassle with him only as long as you and he can enjoy each other.

- Remember that hassling is one way to learn about rules.

- Sometimes let *him* establish the rules, and you follow them, too.

- Reread the rules on the game box, or consult *Hoyle's Card Games*. (See "Resources.")

- Create your own game with him, and write down the rules.

- Change your own attitude by visualizing him playing happily and peacefully.

- Breathe deeply and think about what you and he want to accomplish with this time together.

- Give him positive feedback when he follows rules.

Thanks to Nancy Drake,
Suggestion Circle from Walnut Creek, California

5. My child wants to be paid for everything she does around the house. What can I do?

- Children are a part of the family and deserve some of the family resources.

- "Pay" her in some other form, such as with a toy, a new piece of clothing, or a trip to the zoo.

- Explain that you all work together in your family and that everyone does certain household tasks without payment.

- Agree on the chores she will be paid for. Don't pay her if she doesn't do the chore.

- Kids should do household chores, and if we have enough money to pay them, then we do.

- Remember, earning your own money is important.

- Don't pay. Give her an allowance not connected to helping around the house.

- Pay her for some chores and not for others.
  (See also questions 2, 3, and 8.)

Thanks to Darlene Montz,
Suggestion Circle from Yakima, Washington

6. My kids mow lawns and baby-sit. Who decides what they do with the money?

- They do.

- Contract with them to save half and spend half.

- Treat all family income as belonging to the family—kids' income, too. They add to the family pot, and take it out according to need.

- Show them how to budget by showing them how you budget for family expenses. Then expect them to contribute some of their money toward some important family purchase.

- It's OK to insist that they use a portion of their earnings to support their needs for clothing, food, school supplies, and so on.

- Remember that they will learn from making purchasing mistakes with their own money, especially if they can talk it over with you.

- Read *Teaching Your Child About Money*, by Chris Snyder. (See "Resources.")

(See also "Structuring for Success.")

Thanks to Judy Popp,
Suggestion Circle from Yakima, Washington

7. My eight-year-old son doesn't get ready on time in the morning. What can I do?

- You schedule the morning routine, and then walk him through it a few times to be sure he knows what he needs to do.

- Discuss with him why he is not getting ready. He may not want to go to school. Find out why.

- The night before, tell him that you love him and will look forward to seeing him in the morning.

- Teach him how to set a timer or the clock radio so it will go on at the time he should be *finished* dressing.

- Call him only once. Let him be late and take the consequences: walk to school or miss the day of school with no TV.

- Have him do more of his getting ready at night.

- Send him to bed half an hour earlier each week until he gets enough sleep to wake easily in the morning.

- Wake him with a back rub.

- Establish rewards for getting up on time.

- Plan to do something together the first ten minutes of the morning. Read a book together, exercise, make pancakes.

  (See also questions 18, 34, 37, and 39.)

  Thanks to Barb Kobe,
  Suggestion Circle from Crystal, Minnesota

8. My daughter will not clean her room. What can I do?

- Take away a privilege. Having one's own room is itself a privilege in some families.

- Offer instruction on room cleaning and how to break the task into little steps—making the bed, picking up clothing, and so on.

- Close the door.

- Some things are more fun to do when you have help. You could team up and share jobs around the house.

- Let her have a "messy corner" in her room. The rest of the room is to be neat.

- Reward her when she keeps her room clean several days in a row.

- Tell her that she is a good housekeeper whenever she demonstrates this skill.

- With your daughter, draw up a plan for redecorating the room later and for making it look a little nicer now.

- Tell her that you will clean her room if she will clean the living room.
- Give her an "I will clean your room one time" certificate. She may discover that she likes a clean room.

(See also questions 2 and 5.)

Thanks to Nancy O'Hara,
Suggestion Circle from Minneapolis, Minnesota

9. At what age can my older child be expected to baby-sit our younger ones or the neighbor's kids, and how can I help him be successful?

- We let our child start sitting for the next-door neighbor at age eleven, but only when we were home in case she needed help.
- Let him know you are available to answer questions or to help in an emergency.
- Help him with suggestions and by example. Show him how by visiting him when he's baby-sitting the first couple of times.
- Make a list with him of "important rules for baby-sitting," such as:

  1) No phone calls.
  2) No visitors.
  3) This is a job; treat it like one. Get phone numbers and parental direction.
  4) Follow safety guidelines.

- Ten is too young to baby-sit. You can help him out by not allowing it.

- Send him to a baby-sitting clinic.

- Ask him to listen to Clarke's tapes on child development, The Wonderful Busy Ones and The Terrific Twos, and then have him tell you what he heard about good care for each age child. (See "Resources.")

- Let him start by being the sitter for the younger ones in your home for half an hour while you are there to answer questions. Set the timer. As soon as he begins to learn the rules, start to pay him.

- Call your local child protection agency for guidelines on this.

Thanks to Kathy Bliven Huseby,
Suggestion Circle from Minneapolis, Minnesota

Chapter 2

Discipline

10. What is the difference between discipline and punishment?

- Discipline says, "Stop. Do something else instead." Punishment says, "You did something wrong, and you are bad!"

- Discipline sets the child up for success next time. Punishment focuses on failure.

- If there is physical hurt, it is punishment.

- Discipline is something that shows consequences but is not as severe as punishment.

- Discipline does not expect more than a child this age can do. Punishment often does.

- Discipline is learning the right and wrong of life. Punishment is the negative side of discipline.

- Discipline addresses the *act* as wrong. Punishment addresses the *person* as wrong.

- Discipline has a good chance of being effective. The results of punishment are unpredictable.

- Discipline comes from thought, and punishment comes from anger.

- Punishment is being disciplined without knowing what's expected of you.

- If the parent feels gleeful or vengeful, it's punishment.

(See also questions 19, 90, and "How to Make and Enforce Rules.")

Thanks to Christine Ternand,
Suggestion Circle from Saint Paul, Minnesota

11. What can I do instead of hitting, yelling, or verbally abusing my children?

- Get professional counseling.
- Leave the room. Later talk to the child about why you were angry.
- Take a parenting class.
- Read James Windell's *Discipline.* (See "Resources.")
- Count to twenty.
- Use a fuss box. (See the section entitled "Fuss Box.")
- Tell your angry thoughts to a tape recorder and play it back. What did you hear?
- Close your eyes and think about the positive qualities of the child; then share your positive thoughts with him.
- Hit a pillow, if that is what you tell your children to do when they are angry.
- Be aware of why you are angry, breathe deeply, and think.
- Tell the child that you are angry, why you are angry, and calmly discuss what to do about it.
- Call your local crisis hot line.

(See also questions 3, 10, 19, 90, "Common Pitfalls," and "Keeping School-Age Children Safe.")

Thanks to Deane Gradous,
Suggestion Circle from Saint Paul, Minnesota

12. What do I do when my child says, "I won't, and you can't make me"?

- Offer options instead of ultimatums.

- Make it clear which rules are bendable and which she has to follow.

- Give the kid some consequences.

- Establish parent and child roles; make sure your child knows you are in charge.

- Say, "Look, that's the way I felt about grocery shopping this week, but I did it anyway. People have to do some things they don't like."

- Say, "I hear you say 'I won't'; what do you say 'I will' to?"

- Acknowledge her saying a loud and strong no. Remember, this is what we want her to say when someone offers her drugs.

- When it's a nonnegotiable rule say, "Are you going to do it yourself, or am I going to help you?"

- Maybe the child is saying, "Listen to me—I want to be heard!"

- Check out your language or your tone of voice. Maybe you asked her to do the thing in a way that assumed she would be rebellious.

- Don't say, "Will you . . . ?" unless no is an OK response. If you want her to do something, tell her to do it; don't ask.

(See also question 47.)

Thanks to Deane Gradous,
Suggestion Circle from Saint Paul, Minnesota

13. My child is using lots of dirty words, and I disapprove. What can I do?

- Check your feelings as to why the words are "hot."

- Ask him to use nonsense words instead.

- Tell the child how bad you feel being around such language.

- Don't make a big fuss over this, as it adds importance to the words. Also, don't use them yourself.

- Calmly state that you don't like to hear those words, and suggest he go into his room to say them so you don't have to hear them.

- Point out your disapproval of this language to him initially, and then ignore it. It may be just a way of getting a reaction from you. If the problem continues, ask him if he has a reason for using words you don't like.

- Say, "If you use those words around me, I will expect you to . . . " Then set a consequence you can live with, such as having your child list four ways he could have said what he said without dirty words.

- Tell him about your family's values, and expect him to respect them.

- Totally ignore the words for one month and see if he stops using them.

  (See also questions 17 and 45.)

Thanks to Darlene Montz,
Suggestion Circle from Yakima, Washington

14. My children, ages five and seven, ride their bikes in the street. It is not safe. What can I do?

- Tell them why you are concerned, and tell them where they *can* ride.

- If the local police department offers classes, take the kids to a class on bike safety.

- Go over safety rules about how and when to ride in the street.

- Set definite rules, and take the bikes away for one day the first time a rule is broken, two days the second time, and so on.

- Go riding with them to teach them safety rules for riding in streets. Then continue to go with them occasionally to see if they are obeying the rules.

- Have the whole family ride on the bike paths in parks.

- While you show them how to maintain and clean their bikes, which helps teach them the value of the bikes, talk with them about safety rules and the value of their own bodies.

- Insist that your children wear helmets anyplace they ride.

  (See also questions 3 and 10.)

Thanks to Bernice Brotherton,
Suggestion Circle from Saint Paul, Minnesota

15. I want suggestions for ways to help my daughter, age seven, to be a better listener when I ask her to do something or when I give her directions.

- Touch her arm or hand to get her attention before you talk to her.

- Make sure you have eye contact.

- Sometimes talk to her at her eye level.

- Try drawing pictures to remind her, or writing the directions in words she can read.

- Ask her to repeat back to you what you have just told her. If that doesn't work, ask her what she felt or saw in her mind's eye.

- Reward her when she follows directions.

- At the end of the day, during her quiet time before bed, tell her some of the ways you saw her being a good listener.

- Have the doctor check her hearing. Remember, when she has a cold or sinus infection, her hearing may be temporarily impaired.

- Affirm her listening well when you notice her doing it.

- Seven-year-olds are more interested in *doing* than in listening to directions. Sometimes it is OK to let her go ahead without directions and to let her learn from that.

- Let her look away, or ask her if she wants you to write out the task.

(See also questions 49 and 77.)

Thanks to Nat Houtz,
Suggestion Circle from Seattle, Washington

16. My kids snack a lot, and then they aren't hungry at mealtime. I want them to eat meals at the table. How do other families handle this problem?

- Set clear rules about times when they can and can't snack.

- Try having dinner earlier.

- Don't buy junk food. Keep fresh cleaned vegetables in the refrigerator. Snacking on them will do less harm to their appetite for dinner.

- Serve apples, and make a rule as to the latest time they can eat them.

- Help them plan a game or fun activity to do before meal-time so that they don't snack out of boredom.

- Consider serving five small meals a day instead of three large ones.

- Work out a list of foods acceptable for snacks, and buy only those.

- Have a family conference to discuss how to resolve the problem.

- Hold a family Suggestion Circle. (See "How to Lead a Suggestion Circle.")

- Have the kids help plan the menus. Have them help cook the meals.

  (See also question 66.)

Thanks to Kitty Lindall,
Suggestion Circle from Prior Lake, Minnesota

17. My son's best friend won't follow our house rules. What shall I do?

- Confront the friend. List your important house rules for him, and tell him that everyone in your house follows these rules.

- Explain the rules again. Then tell him that if he does not obey your house rules, he will be sent home and cannot return until the next day. Follow through with this.

- Be clear about the rules so that both your son and the friend know what they are. If you like the friend, let him know that you do.

- In a friendly way, explain that your house rules may be different from his. Tell him that you expect him to follow your rules at your house.

- Post the rules.

- Say "Good job!" when the friend follows a rule.

- Use this opportunity to evaluate your house rules and see if they are reasonable.

- Let your son know you expect him to be part of the solution.

- Kids who follow the rules get jelly beans.

Thanks to Mary Paananen,
Suggestion Circle from Seattle, Washington

18. How can I get my kids, ages five and seven, to go to bed on time?

- Start "ready-for-bed" time early enough so they can read by themselves or play with a toy for fifteen minutes before lights out.

- Half an hour before bedtime ring a signal bell.

- Set a timer for bedtime. When the bell rings, they are to turn it off and go to bed.

- Tell them you need some time for yourself.

- Don't give them chocolate or other caffeinated or sweet foods in the evening.

- Explain about sleep and its benefits. Discuss how many hours are needed.

- Spend some time with each child just before bed.

- Routine is important; be consistent.

- Quiet time is important. Read or talk; don't roughhouse, tease, or tickle just before bed.

- Have them spend ten to thirty minutes before bedtime doing a special project for themselves.

- Make a game of "everyone who's in bed in five minutes wins." Then firmly put anyone back in bed who gets up.

- Put a paper clock next to the real clock, and when the hands match, it is time for bed.

Thanks to Eveline Goodall,
Suggestion Circle from Calgary, Alberta, Canada

19. What can I do when I realize that I am doing things to my kids that my parents did to me and that I vowed I would never do?

- Notice all the ways in which you are copying your parents. Keep the ones that are positive. Change only those that are not positive.

- If you are doing something that you hated as a child but now realize is necessary, accept it. I have told my kids, "Wow, I sound just like my mother. How do you like that? I used to hate it when she said that! But it *is* important!"

- Count to ten or say the ABCs. Then apologize and think of a better way.

- Get therapy.

- Apologize to your children when you have used an old negative method. Talk about how you will handle such a situation next time.

- Tell your kids what your parents did well, and ask your kids to tell you what you do well.

- Take a parenting class. Try out new ways of disciplining every week until you find ways that you like.

- Write down a list of alternative ways to discipline. Then consult your list before disciplining.
- Study Elizabeth Crary's *Without Spanking or Spoiling*. (See "Resources.")

  (See also question 11 and "How to Make and Enforce Rules.")

  Thanks to Sandra Sittko,
  Suggestion Circle from Saint Paul, Minnesota

Chapter 3

Brothers and Sisters, Friends and Peers

20. My child is putting down the younger children in the family and bossing them around. What should a parent do?

- Say, "I don't like what you are saying. Please say something positive or leave the room."

- Hold up a "Stop" sign.

- Make a "no put-down" rule. Post it, and insist the whole family observe it.

- Read Claude Steiner's *Warm Fuzzy Tale* to all of them. (See "Resources.")

- Send her for a time-out. (See "Time-Out" in Appendixes.)

- Put your arm around her. Say in a pleasant tone, "In this family, we don't put each other down. We help each other. How can I help you?"

- Show her the affirmations. Ask her which of them she'd rather tell her siblings. (See "Developmental Affirmations for All Ages.")

- Offer love to *all* the children.

- Teach the children to *fall* down when they hear a *put-*down. It is hard to continue put-downs when everyone else is lying on the floor playing dead.

- Ask her to teach the other children instead of bossing them.

- When the older one is to be in charge, tell the younger ones how long it will last.

- When giving the older one the responsibility of watching the younger ones, give her guidelines, and explain how to take care of them with skill.

- Send her to baby-sitting school.

  (See also question 60.)

Thanks to Judi Salts,
Suggestion Circle from Yakima, Washington

21. What can I do when my six- and eight-year-olds tattle on each other?

- Ask the librarian to find some books about tattling. Read the stories before bedtime, or ask the children to read them when you are together in the car.

- Sit down with them and explain the difference between tattling and reporting. Reporting is giving you important information that you should have.

- When the tattling is about a health or safety issue, listen.

- Tell them they can tattle into a tape recorder if they need to tattle. They can erase the tape when they want to listen to something that's more fun.

- Tell the children you want to hear both sides.

- Clap your hands over your ears.

- Give each child lots of attention when he or she is not tattling. This behavior may be a bid for attention.

- Tell the children that they have a problem and that they can decide what to do about it.
- You could get another adult to play-act tattling in front of the children. Say, "This is tattling, and I won't listen to it."

(See also question 46.)

Thanks to Melanie Weiss,
Suggestion Circle from Bellevue, Washington

22. My daughter complains that she is tired of sharing a bedroom with her younger sister. She wants her own room.

- Say, "You could have the guest room, but then you'd have to move out every time we have company or when exchange students come."
- Remodel the basement, and include another bedroom in your plans.
- Place a desk, chest of drawers, or bookcase so that it divides the room.
- Ask, "What do you suggest? Do you have a better way of arranging the bedrooms we have?"
- Suggest that they arrange to spend an hour alone in the bedroom each day for private time.
- Give the older sister a "special" nook in another part of the house.
- Find out what the problem is. A need for privacy? Time alone? Personal safety? Safety for her belongings? No place for friends? Then decide what to do.

Thanks to Rosemary and Cy Rief,
Suggestion Circle from Yakima, Washington

23. My seven- and nine-year-olds are too competitive. What can I do to downplay the competition?

- Plan activities for them that take cooperation between two people.

- Look for differences in each child to praise and affirm. Get them to compete in separate areas.

- Read Faber and Mazlish's *Siblings Without Rivalry.* (See "Resources.")

- Stress each child's individuality, and avoid trying to make things fair and equal. Spend some time alone with each of them.

- Check out how you and your spouse are relating in front of them. Do you cooperate, or do you compete?

- Get the *New Games Book,* by Andrew Fluegelman, and use it. (See "Resources.")

- Get the whole family involved in a cooperative venture, and talk about the importance of working together.

- Don't compare them. Say, "You do that well!" Do not say, "You do that better than your sister."

- Give some privileges and responsibilities to the nine-year-old that the other has to wait until age nine for.

- Read *Kids Can Cooperate,* by Elizabeth Crary. (See "Resources.")

Thanks to Jean Clarke,
Suggestion Circle from Plymouth, Minnesota

24. What can I do when my son and daughter ask, "Why do *I* have to do the dishes?" In other words, why not the other one?

- Change the chore list every week.

- Say, "You must do the dishes now. We will talk about family chores later this evening."

- Ask, "What do you think you could do about this problem?" Listen well. They might have a better idea.

- Center your body and say, "You know whose responsibility the dishes are this week."

- Suggest that they trade chores with each other. Remind them that their jobs must be done, no matter who does them.

- Sometimes when all the chores are finished quickly and well, do a special family activity.

(See also questions 2 and 8.)

Thanks to Kitty Lindall,
Suggestion Circle from Shakopee, Minnesota

25. My kids fight a lot. What can I do?

- Say, "I'm not interested in listening to you fight. Please leave the area."

- Set a rule that arguments are to be sung. My kids ended up laughing before many minutes were up.

- Stop them. Clarify your rules about name-calling and hitting. Determine consequences and then follow through.

- Try whispering "I love you" in the ear of each child, and see if that helps.

- If they are harming one another physically, stop them.

- Separate them. Invite them to write down what they think the fight is about. Then invite them to come together and settle the issue.

- If you have been mediating, now try ignoring the fight.

- Play often with them with lots of body contact. Give hugs. Perhaps they need to be touched.

- Read *He Hit Me First*, by Louise Bates Ames et al. (See "Resources.")

- Have a family meeting, and ask the children if they need anything from other family members to help them live more peaceably.

- Stop the fight, and have them each report one thing they value about each other.

  (See also questions 23 and 36.)

  Thanks to Harold Nordeman,
  Suggestion Circle from Cincinnati, Ohio

26. How can I deal with my seven-year-old who wants all the privileges that are given to my ten-year-old?

- Set the rules and privileges for each child, and stick with them.

- Explain about age differences. Go back to when they were one and four. The four-year-old could talk, the one-year-old could not. Explain that the seven-year-old does not have all the privileges or all the responsibilities that the ten-year-old has.

- Give lots of love to both of them. Be careful not to fan the competition. Say, "As you get older, you get more responsibilities, and with those come privileges."

- Look at each child as an individual. When a child is capable of a responsibility, let him or her be responsible. Privileges come after responsibilities are handled well.

- Say, "I'm pretty sure you know what privileges and re-sponsibilities are appropriate for each of you. You don't have to like the rules about this, but you do have to follow them."

- Worry about safety and development and each child's needs, and don't worry about what's "fair."

- Say, "It may not seem fair, but that's the way it is."

(See also question 23.)

Thanks to Deane Gradous,
Suggestion Circle from Minnetonka, Minnesota

27. My children insist on wearing designer clothes. Virtually all their friends have the "right" shoes and jeans. These clothes don't fit my pocketbook, and I don't think they are appropriate.

- Have your children become a part of the family discussion about finances.

- Tell the children what you will spend for jeans. Let them make up the difference from their allowances or earnings.

- Read David Elkind's *The Hurried Child* for support in not pushing your children to grow up too fast. (See "Resources.")

- Have them figure out ways to earn money in order to buy the clothing they want.

- Tell the children that each can have one designer item a season. Set a price limit, and let them choose.

- Have a discussion about values and how we judge others by their clothing.

- Teach them how to shop discount houses and sales.
- Give them compliments for their personality and not just for their appearance. Clothing doesn't make the person.
- Send them to a school where all the kids wear uniforms. (See also questions 6 and 51.)

Thanks to Lois White,
Suggestion Circle from Minnetonka, Minnesota

28. I think my child is in a group at school that isn't good for her. What shall I do?

- Talk to the teacher and other parents, and see how they perceive the situation.
- Talk with the child. Stress values. Say, "It's OK to have all kinds of friends, but don't hurt yourself or others."
- Model the behavior you want. What kind of values do you and your friends espouse?
- Try to find out what her values are. If this group is really bad, consider changing schools.
- Encourage her to get involved in a sport.
- Give the affirmations for Structure. (See "Affirmations for Growth—Structure.")
- Encourage activity in positive groups. You could become a scout leader or a Sunday school teacher and involve her there.
- Don't condemn her friends before you talk to her and find out something about these friends. You may be wrong.
- Encourage her to invite her friends to a party. See if you can learn what she values in them.

- Invite her friends over to play the "Love Game." (See "Other Learning Materials Available.")

Thanks to Linda Buranen,
Suggestion Circle from Plymouth, Minnesota

29. What do I do when I tell my eleven-year-old he has done something well, and he says, "The kids say you shouldn't brag. Cool kids don't like bragging."

- Tell him, "Feeling good about what you have done is not bragging." Teach him the difference, and keep on praising him.

- Compliments are not bragging, but telling someone you received a compliment could be considered bragging. Tell him to choose when and where to celebrate his wins.

- I would begin by building self-esteem with Being affirmations: "You are neat just because you are you." "I love you." As he becomes comfortable with these messages, he will gradually accept recognition or praise for "doing" well. (See "Developmental Affirmations for All Ages.")

- Say, "If you don't want to tell the kids when you do something well, don't. But tell me, and be sure to tell yourself."

- Say, "Keep looking for a friend you can brag with. Someday, somewhere, you will find that person, and then you will have a special friend. It is important to be proud of yourself."

- Have him make a list of ten things that he likes about himself and share it with you or some other trusted adult.

(See also question 59.)

Thanks to Linda Buranen,
Suggestion Circle from Plymouth, Minnesota

30. Our six-year-old idolizes another boy and wants to do everything and have the same things as his idol. What should a parent say or do?

- Say, "I notice that you have a friend you admire. It's great to have a friend you admire lots."

- Say, "Each of us is different. You are Matt, and he is Scott."

- Say, "You can think about what Scott does before you decide to do it." Offer the affirmations for Structure. (See "Affirmations for Growth—Structure.")

- Value your son's requests on their own merit. Tell him how you decide. Whether or not the other boy has something should not be the deciding factor in whether your son gets to have it.

- Make some firm family rules about what people do, and stick with them.

- Talk about some people *you* admire and why you admire them.

- With him, find one thing that he can do like the other boy and one thing that he can do just because he is himself, growing up in his own family.

- Take both boys on an outing, and give each positive messages for their uniqueness.

- Be sure that the other boy is a good influence on your son. If he isn't, encourage your son to look for new friends.

Thanks to Ellen Peterson,
Suggestion Circle from Orinda, California

31. How can I comfort my child when she feels that no one likes her and no one wants to play with her?

- Tell your child that you will take her and a friend some-place fun. Show her different ways to invite friends to do things. If this doesn't work, try again with another child or several children, but only take them one-on-one so they can talk and get to know each other.

- Give her lots of affirmations for Being. (See "Developmental Affirmations for All Ages.")

- Empathize with her: "Sounds like you are feeling left out." Then listen to her some more.

- Invite her to make bread with you. While you knead, talk about how sometimes your friends want to play with you and sometimes they don't.

- Challenge her thinking. Ask her to tell you three ways the kids show they like her and three ways they show they don't like her.

- Tell her that you believe she will find ways to solve this problem.

- Say, "Wait until after dinner and call Katy again. Maybe she will be home by then."

- Say, "Go get the cards, and we will play a game. Practice with me how to play cards and be a friend."

(See also questions 42, 59, and 60.)

Thanks to Rosemary and Cy Rief,
Suggestion Circle from Yakima, Washington

32. My daughter won't play with boys because she says they have "boy germs." What can I do?

- Don't fuss about it; allow her to have her own feelings on the matter. Realize that this is a phase.

- Hassle her gently. Say, "They do? What kind?"

- Ask her if she has "girl germs."

- Tell her that she can play with boys when she is ready.

- Ask her what "boy germs" are. Does this stand for some distorted sexual information? If so, find the source.

- Take a look at your own friendships. Do you have friends of the opposite sex?

- Tell her, "I remember when I thought that. Now I think that boys and men are just as valuable and as much fun as girls and women."

- Leave her alone. She'll decide when to have boy playmates. I wouldn't force her to play with boys.

- Explain that boys and girls are both important, and let her choose her own friends.

- Encourage her to play with girls. She needs to accept and appreciate her own sex before she can accept and appreciate a person of the opposite sex.

Thanks to Sandra Sittko,
Suggestion Circle from Saint Paul, Minnesota

Chapter 4

School

33. My sixth-grader is in a new school, and he is having trouble adjusting. How can I help him?

- Identify more specifically the reason he is having trouble. Make sure you understand the problem before you try to solve it.

- If he is not caught up with his class in some subject, get a tutor.

- Find out what clubs and after-school activities are available, and let him choose one or two to try out.

- Discuss ways to make new friends.

- Schedule fun activities, and say it's OK to invite a friend.

- Meet with the teachers and ask them for ideas.

- Meet some of the other parents. When you can, arrange for him to meet new kids outside of school.

- Take time to listen each night. He might do better if he can talk things out with you.

- Give him three more weeks.

- Purchase *Goodbye, House,* by Ann Banks and Nancy Evans, and go through it together or separately. Perhaps you and he are grieving the loss of his old friends and school and just need some more time to adjust. (See "Resources.")

(See also questions 31, 42, and 59.)

Thanks to Nancy Delin,
Suggestion Circle from Chaska, Minnesota

34. My child has been acting up in school. His name has been "on the board" so many times that the teacher called home to talk to me. What can I do?

- Tell your child that this is not what you expected, and ask what you can do to help.

- Offer him the Identity and Power affirmations. Support his power. (See "Developmental Affirmations for All Ages.")

- Have a conference with the teacher and the child. Offer to help them both get this problem resolved.

- Sometimes children act up at school because of problems at home. Is something different at home?

- Ask his teacher what he does well. Ask her to write his name on the board for doing that well.

- Does he follow the rules at home? If not, build in consequences. What he learns at home will help him at school.

- Make a contract with the teacher, stating the consequences for your son if he does not follow school rules. Tell him to follow the rules at school.

- Ask him how he feels about having his name on the board and what he plans to do about it.

- Expect him to think before he does things. He can learn to keep himself out of trouble.

  (See also question 65.)

  Thanks to Toni Drucker,
  Suggestion Circle from Lafayette, California

35. My child won't do her homework. Taking away TV doesn't make any difference.

- Set aside a time of the day when adults and kids do quiet work together at the table. Parents do their work, and kids do theirs. If she doesn't have homework, she can read or do other quiet work.

- With her, set homework time and playtime and stick to it. Invite her to show you her homework when she is done.

- After school, offer her a snack, ask her if she has any assignments, and tell her to do her homework right away.

- Don't bail her out. Homework is the child's responsibility.

- Often homework is no big deal in terms of the time needed to finish it. She may, however, need your support in learning to do new things and in how to organize. (See "Structuring for Success.")

- Change the pattern at home if she gets a lot of attention for *not* doing her homework or if she only gets help when she's in a crisis. Give her energy and attention when she is doing her work.

- Celebrate successful work by telling others about it and by putting it on the refrigerator.

(See also questions 38, 39, 40, and 59.)

Thanks to Margo Tobias,
Suggestion Circle from Orinda, California

36. Our daughter is coming home from school looking for a fight, and she often finds one. What can I do to help her?

- Ask her if she needs more time with you or your partner.

- She may be having school problems. Outline the problem with the teacher, and work together with the teacher and your child toward a solution.

- Spend time just with her.

- She may be getting negative attention. Tell her, "I'm getting tired of your behavior. Is there something we can talk about to help you with it?"

- Talk with her about her anger or frustration.

- Is she getting enough sleep and eating right?

- Tell her, "Go to your room and settle down."

- Set aside time when she is not fighting, talk with her about her behavior.

- Ask her if she is tense. Teach her songs and exercises to help her relax.

- Teach her to use the fuss box. (See the section entitled "The Fuss Box.")

- Refuse to spar with her.

- Play Gesme's *Ups and Downs with Feelings* games with her. (See "Other Learning Materials Available.")

(See also question 25.)

Thanks to Nancy O'Hara,
Suggestion Circle from Minneapolis, Minnesota

37. My six-year-old daughter is tearful and fearful of a teacher who "taps" kids in class. How can I address this problem at an interview with the teacher?

- Feel confident of your rights as a parent, and don't stop until you are fully satisfied about the physical and psychological safety of your daughter. Talk with the teacher and then the principal, if necessary.

- Affirm yourself for coping with this problem. Also know that other children may be upset.

- Bring up the issue now—don't put it off.

- It is important to talk with your daughter to find out how she feels. Get more information. Make sure she is telling you specifically what the problem is. Give her support.

- Share with the teacher your concern about having to bring up the subject. Treat the teacher with respect but not reverence.

- Check with other parents about the situation.

- Don't fly off the handle with the teacher.

- Role-play the interview with a friend before doing it. First play you, then the teacher.

- Find out if hitting children is permitted in the school in your area. Be clear about your right to protect your child from physical abuse. You may need to check out other schools and their discipline policies.

(See also "Signs of Abuse and Neglect.")

Thanks to Eveline Goodall,
Suggestion Circle from Calgary, Alberta, Canada

38. My child should be getting better grades. What shall I do?

- Spend time with him reading and playing academic games. Stop when it is not fun.

- Ask him what he thinks about school and about learning. Listen carefully. Explain that you want him to do his best but that this does not mean he needs to be perfect.

- Tell him you will give him an agreed-on reward if his grades start improving.

- Affirm him for Thinking and Doing. (See "Developmental Affirmations for All Ages.")

- Have him checked for learning disabilities. If he is gifted and bored, seek out enrichment opportunities.

- If this is a sudden change, make certain it is not a symptom of abuse or of drugs.

- Do not help with homework. That responsibility belongs to your child and the teacher.

- Make a rule that homework comes before play or television.

- The teacher's style of teaching may not match your child's learning needs. Find out if there is a teacher with another style of teaching who would be a better match for your son.

- Spend ten to fifteen minutes a day with him using an attitude and study-habits course such as *Straight Talk*, by Robert Maidment. (See "Resources.")

(See also questions 33, 35, and 40.)

Thanks to Harold Nordeman,
Suggestion Circle from Cincinnati, Ohio

39. My child worries constantly that she's not going to get her daily assignments done.

- Be sure she gets approval for the fun things she does when she is not doing homework.

- Schedule homework time with her, and check at intervals to see what she has accomplished. Do *not* permit homework to be done at any other time.

- Find out what happens at school if a daily assignment is not done.

- Ask yourself if you have set up your life to work all the time and have little fun. If so, begin to enjoy life more yourself.

- Doing accomplishes more than worrying. Help her start doing so she'll have less time for worrying.

- Is she trying to be a perfect student? Will your family accept mistakes?

- Perhaps she has so many responsibilities at home that she has trouble getting to her homework.

- Is she using her homework as a way to get out of doing chores?

- Give her lots of unconditional love.

- Ask her teacher if she is having a problem finishing things at school and so must do them at home.

(See also questions 7, 35, 38, and 40.)

Thanks to Maggie Lawrence,
Suggestion Circle from Seattle, Washington

40. What can I say to my son when he puts himself down because he hasn't done well in his schoolwork?

- Give him compliments about the things he does well.

- Say "How come you are talking mean about someone I love?"

- Tell him, "You don't have to get A's for me to love you."

- Say "Do your best in school, and that is fine."

- Say over and over, "I like you the way you are, and I like to see you grow."

- Show him ways in which you think, try new things, make mistakes, and change.

- Explain, "Everyone makes mistakes. Mistakes don't make you a bad person. They tell you what to improve."

- Give him lots of love and encourage him to think about what kind of student he wants to be.

- Say "We don't hurt people, and you are a very important person."

- Say "Tell me three things you like about yourself."

- Disagree with him.

- Get Gesme's *Paper People*, and encourage your son to choose positive sweatshirt messages. (See "Resources.")

  (See also questions 29, 35, 38, 39, and 59.)

Thanks to Annette Bodmer,
Suggestion Circle from Burnsville, Minnesota

41. I know my child needs special help from the school counselor or a tutor, but my wife won't hear of it.

- Do what is best for the child.

- Set up a meeting with your wife, your child, and your child's counselor.

- Tell your child, "I love you. You will get the special help you deserve."

- Ask your wife to think about why she objects and to discuss it. Perhaps she attaches some sort of stigma to getting help. Talk about all the ways people must rely on other people just to live.

- Go to a minister or doctor for help on how to handle your differences with your wife.

- Show and tell your spouse in many ways, "You are lovable and capable and not a failure because our child needs help."

- Ask a relative or friend who has used counseling to talk to your wife and reassure her that it is OK for your kid to get special help.

- Have the child tested to make sure she needs the help. Ask your wife to read the reports.

Thanks to Mary Kay Truitt,
Suggestion Circle from Saint Paul, Minnesota

Chapter 5

Skill Building

42. How can I get my child to try new things?

- Try new things yourself.

- Take him to art and science museums.

- Rehearse new experiences with him. You could use puppets or dolls to role-play the new activity.

- Send him to camp now and to Outward Bound later.

- Tell him a story about a child or yourself as a child who was scared and went on to succeed.

- Read old myths, fairy tales, and biographies to him.

- Affirm his past successful experiences when he tried something new.

- Stop talking about it with him, and in three months, check to see if he is trying more new things.

- Do some new things together.

- Instead of sending him off for the day with a "Take care of yourself," you could say, "Take a chance today."

- Point out people taking risks.

- Affirm his strengths and capabilities.

- Acknowledge risk-taking behavior whenever he exhibits it.

  (See also question 33 and "Coaching: An Essential Skill.")

  Thanks to Sandra Sittko,
  Suggestion Circle from Saint Louis, Missouri

43. I want to make sure my child learns to use a computer. What are some ways I can do that?

- Ask her if she is ready for summer computer camp.

- Hire a high school computer whiz to tutor her.

- People can learn to use computers at any age. Don't hurry her.

- Look at the school program. She should learn to use a computer at school.

- Buy a computer, learn how to use it yourself, and encourage the whole family to learn.

- Games teach computer familiarity. Go on from there.

- When your child bugs you for a computer, rent one for a month.

Thanks to Jean Clarke,
Suggestion Circle from Plymouth, Minnesota

44. It is important to me that my kids write thank-you notes. How can I help make it less of a chore for my nine- and twelve-year-olds?

- Buy thank-you notes, and let them just sign their names.

- Don't correct what they write.

- Let them telephone their thanks.

- Tell them they don't have to like the gift; they just have to say thanks.

- Encourage them to be creative and design their own cards.

- Buy fun stationery.

- Look for opportunities to send or give thank-you notes to *them*.

- Let them record thank-you tapes or send thank-you pictures.

- Do your thank-you notes or letters while they do theirs, and have a family "thank-you note affair."

- Make a family rule that thank-you notes or calls go out within three days after the gift is received.

Thanks to Bobbi Mlekodaj,
Suggestion Circle from Coon Rapids, Minnesota

45. My son sometimes acts in ways that turn people off. What can I do to help him eliminate these behaviors?

- Catch him being effective, and praise him for it.

- Model the desired behavior.

- Challenge the child after he has turned people off, and listen to his responses.

- Don't protect him from the consequences of his behavior.

- Describe your feelings about what happened, and suggest alternatives. "I felt mad while you were making fun of Lynn's ideas. Try telling what you think without mentioning anyone else."

- Discuss the logical consequences of his behavior, saying, "People may not want to be with you." And point out his responsibility for his choices: "Only you can decide how you act."

- Ask him how he would feel if someone had acted that way around him.

- Ask him what he could have done differently.

- Say, "You are smart. You can think of other ways to get what you want."

- Borrow a tape recorder (audio or video) from the library. Tape his behavior, let him listen, and ask him if he'd like to change anything.

(See also questions 13, 15, 25, and 48.)

Thanks to Bobbi Mlekodaj,
Suggestion Circle from Plymouth, Minnesota

46. My twelve-year-old gossips maliciously. What can I say or do to discourage this behavior?

- Remind her that a gossipy mouth can get the whole person in trouble.

- Give her the Being affirmations. (See "Developmental Affirmations for All Ages.")

- Tell her the story about gossip. Gossip is a person who opens a bag of feathers on a hill. The feathers randomly blow every which way and reach people Gossip did not intend for them to reach. What's more, all the feathers can never be recovered.

- Ask her to think about how she feels when someone gossips about her.

- Pick a regularly scheduled library night out. Help her find other things to talk about.

- Whenever you hear her gossiping about someone, ask her to make two positive statements about that person.

- Tell her that you will be glad when she changes the way she talks.

- Ask her to find another way to talk with people.

- Give her lots of love. Let her know that she is important to you as a person, not for everything she does.

- Set aside ten minutes, and insist that she tell you *all* the gossip. Then refuse to listen to gossip at any other time of the day.

(See also questions 21, 45, and 49.)

Thanks to Becky Monson,
Suggestion Circle from Plymouth, Minnesota

47. When my son doesn't do something right, he has a tantrum, and he throws his eyeglasses—even in gym class. They are getting broken very often. What can I do about him?

- Why does he get angry in his classes and in gym? *Investigate!*

- Have a "cost" for broken glasses: no movies because he can't see, and part of his allowance goes to help pay for the glasses, and so on.

- Talk to him about anger being an OK feeling. Have him come and tell you when he has dealt with anger appropriately.

- Eight-year-olds can recycle two-year-old stuff. Tell him it's OK to feel angry but not OK to throw glasses. Give him lots of nurturing. (See the affirmations for Thinking in "Developmental Affirmations for All Ages.")

- Make him earn the money to pay for them.

- Let him use the fuss box when he is angry (see "The Fuss Box"). Then get him to finish a project that is less than perfect and accept it that way.

- Find out where the pressure is coming from for him to be perfect, and get it turned off.

- Empathize with him and allow him to be frustrated. Piaget says that when children go from stage to stage, there is a period of frustration, and the child needs to cope with this. The parent should not solve the problem or take away the frustration. (See "Resources.")

(See also questions 12, 15, and 90.)

Thanks to Roxy Chuchna,
Suggestion Circle from Albert Lea, Minnesota

48. My ten-year-old son was caught stealing seventeen dollars from a friend at school. He lied for two days. Now we know about it. How can we confront him?

- Directly.

- Confront him directly and honestly in a civil manner, not as an attack. Let him know that what he did was wrong, and that he will have to make amends for this, but that you still love and care for him. Inspire *guilt,* not *shame.* Read Kaufman's book, *Shame.* (See "Resources.")

- Tell him you know. Discuss a way to pay the money back, including an apology and a fine for stealing and lying.

- Go to the child and tell him what you know. Then say, "Since I am legally and emotionally responsible for you, you are going to take the money back to your friend, and I am going with you." Then do it.

- Confront him with evidence; let him think up his own penalty—perhaps working it off.

- Let him know how important you think it is to be able to trust your friends.

- Read *Teaching Your Children About Money,* by Chris Snyder. (See "Resources.")

(See also questions 10 and 45.)

Thanks to Samara Kemp,
Suggestion Circle from Modesto, California

49. How can I help my children communicate clearly?

- Look at the communication between yourself and other adults. Be sure you are showing them how.

- Ask, "What are you telling me?" Then listen carefully.

- Compliment them when they do communicate clearly.

- Ask, "What are you trying to say to me?"

- Take time and show an openness and willingness to listen. They may need to practice talking, especially if school doesn't encourage self-expression.

- Role-play your situation with them.

- Ask, "Is there something you want me to do besides listen?"

- Use "active listening." Read *Parent Effectiveness Training*, by Thomas Gordon. (See "Resources.")

- Don't trap your children with questions to which you know the answers.

- Encourage them to be responsible for telling how they feel. Don't you tell them. Ask "How do you feel about that?" instead of saying "That makes you mad, doesn't it?"

(See also questions 15 and 77.)

Thanks to Yvonne Gustafson,
Suggestion Circle from Moundsview, Minnesota

50. My child has no sense of humor. How can I help him?

- Take the child to funny places and experience being funny with him.

- Perhaps he has a sense of humor that is different from yours.

- Humor is a creative act that requires permission and nurturing from those around him. Enjoy him and protect him from criticism.

- Catch your child being funny, and compliment him on it.

- Are you able to give humorous messages but not receive them?

- Be sure that your own sense of humor isn't biting.

- When his jokes flop, don't put him down.

- Get him a book on humor.

- Don't mix humor with criticism.

- Look under "novelties" in the yellow pages, and buy props.

- Don't laugh at things that hurt.

- Expose the child to funny people, and let him know that you like them.

- Show your child your own sense of humor.

- Make sure that there is not one child in the family who is labeled the humorous one.

Thanks to Sherri Goldsmith,
Suggestion Circle from Plymouth, Minnesota

Chapter 6

Values and Priorities

51. My ten-year-old wants one of those large, expensive cuddly dolls. I can't stand them. What can I do?

- Remember, ten-year-olds learn from playing with dolls.

- Discuss with her the popularity of these dolls, and explain about "media hype" and about pressure to get what other kids have.

- Get the doll and use this opportunity to share what you know about infant care.

- Discuss your feelings and say no.

- Ask yourself if you dislike the dolls because they might not be good for your child or for some other reason.

- Get the doll if it's so important to her. Getting what is the fad makes your child part of the group. That is important to a ten-year-old.

- A ten-year-old could earn money for a doll.

- If you do buy it, tell her that you did so because you love her and that you will ask her later if it was worth it. Remember, she may learn that it is not important to have what her friends have.

(See also question 27.)

Thanks to Eveline Goodall,
Suggestion Circle from Calgary, Alberta, Canada

52. I don't like the words to the music my twelve-year-old boy listens to. What can I do?

- Tell him, "I'm feeling uncomfortable about the lyrics of the music you listen to. Let's sit down and talk about them."

- Tell him, "I'm not pleased with the words of the music to which you listen. I would like you to listen to music that has positive messages."

- Take him to holiday concerts. Go to church and sing together. Encourage him to sing in choir or learn to play a musical instrument.

- Say, "No, I don't want you to listen to that."

- Ask, "Have you thought about the meaning of the words? Can we discuss them?"

- Offer other types of music for him to listen to, and then invite him to listen with you.

- Ask him to write down the lyrics and read them to you or to another adult. Then ask if those words are what he wants to put into his head.

- Ask him how he thinks people who do what the lyrics say will be living ten years from now.

(See also question 13.)

Thanks to Eveline Goodall,
Suggestion Circle from Calgary, Alberta, Canada

53. My uncle is not expected to live long. We have not talked about death. What do I say, and how can I prepare my children for the funeral?

- Explain it as fully as you can. Tell them older people usually die before younger ones, grandparents before parents.

- Tell them that every living thing in the world dies some-time and that many older people are ready to die when they die.

- Tell them that some people live long lives, and some people live short lives. Uncle has lived a long life.

- You can get some help with your own grieving by reading *Life Is Goodbye—Life Is Hello*, by Alla Bozarth-Campbell. (See "Resources.")

- Take the children to visit your uncle while he is alive.

- Tell them about or have them participate in all the activities of the funeral.

- Encourage them to play funeral with their dolls.

- Express your own sadness. Ask them to comfort you when they feel like it.

- Arrange to give each child something to remember him by.

- Get *My Grandpa Died Today*, by Joan Fassler, *The Dead Bird*, by Margaret Brown, or *When Someone Very Special Dies*, by Marge Heegaard. (See "Resources.")

(See also question 54.)

Thanks to Jean Clarke,
Suggestion Circle from Plymouth, Minnesota

54. My fifteen-year-old nephew committed suicide. Shall we tell the children how he died, or shall we protect them until they are older?

- Be honest with the kids, or they will find out and will wonder why you lied.

- Talk with the kids about what death means to them and how they feel about it.

- Have a discussion with your kids about suicide. This could be an insurance policy against it.

- Use this as an opportunity to discuss feelings about death with your children.

- Help your children look at how suicide affects family and friends.

- Tell them. Encourage them not to blame your nephew as they do not know what was going on in his mind.

- Discuss with the kids the why's of suicide and the alternatives.

- Many adolescents commit suicide. Make sure your children know that suicide does not solve problems.

- Ask your minister, rabbi, or priest to help you talk with your children about suicide.

- Remember that family secrets are usually destructive.

(See also question 53.)

Thanks to Kay Kubes,
Suggestion Circle from Saint Paul, Minnesota

55. My children seem fearful of nuclear war. When they see something about it on TV, they clam up or do something disruptive. What should I do?

- Encourage them to talk about it, and ask how they feel about it.

- Watch the show with them, and ask how they feel about it. If they cry, let them cry.

- Turn off the TV and say, "I want to talk about what we just saw. Will you talk with me?"

- Ask what they have learned about it in school.

- Give them puppets, and ask them to have the puppets tell you how they feel about nuclear war.

- Call your children's school, and ask if it will do something to help all the students with these fears.

- Be sure you feel comfortable talking about it. If you don't, find some friends, or go to a conference where you can practice talking and listening about it.

- Tell them how *you* feel.

- Get Carole Gesme's *Help for Kids! Understanding Your Feelings About the War.* (See "Resources.")

> *Thanks to Jean Clarke,*
> *Suggestion Circle from Wayzata, Minnesota*

56. My sister drinks a lot. My son mentioned it to her, and I'm embarrassed. What can I do?

- I hope you are not embarrassed for your son. You may be embarrassed for your sister or yourself. You can discuss with your child that alcoholism is an illness and that the family can help her.

- Your son did what you should have done before this. Tell him it is OK to notice what is really happening.

- Pat him on the back, tell him it's important to be honest about feelings, and thank him for helping to get this difficult issue into the open.

- This would be a perfect time to have a discussion with your sister.

- Contact Al-Anon, and seek out support for you and your child.

- If you're embarrassed, you may have been brought up to believe the "secrecy rule" about not seeing alcoholism. You need to examine your own rules.

- Talk with the other family members who have been affected by her drinking. As a group, confront her, and offer a plan for what she can do to overcome her problem.

  (See also questions 73 and 74.)

  Thanks to Sandra Sittko,
  Suggestion Circle from Saint Paul, Minnesota

57. Our family has gone to church only sporadically. Now, as parents, we have decided that it is important for the whole family to go to church. The eleven-year-old hassles, and the eight-year-old is scared. What can we do?

- Tell the children, "We have decided that you will go to church because it is important for all of us. You have the choice of sitting quietly in church or going to Sunday school."

- Tell the children, "We have decided that you will go to church for one year because it is an important part of our lives. After church each week, we will discuss your feelings and what you have learned."

- Invite the minister and Sunday school teacher to join you for a social activity or dinner.

- Find out if the kids have any friends who already go to the church you plan to attend. If not, tell them that they can take a friend to Sunday school.

- After church, look for other family activities. Go out for brunch, ice cream, or to the zoo. Make Sunday a family fun day.

- Tell them calmly that you are all going to church once a week, but some weeks they can choose which church activity to attend.

- Visit churches for a month together. At the end of the month, choose a church together.

Thanks to Jeanette Hickman-Kingsley,
Suggestion Circle from Minnetonka, Minnesota

58. I just found out that my eleven-year-old has been going to slasher-movie video parties. These movies show women being abused. The kids play chicken— who can watch the longest. What can I do?

- Talk to your child about why these movies are demeaning and destructive. Share your values and thinking about violence.

- Make sure that there is an adult you trust present at all parties he goes to.

- Ask your child what kids enjoy about the parties. Figure out with him another way for him to have fun.

- Watch a slasher movie with your child, and ask him what he learns about violence from the movie.

- Make it very clear to your child how strongly you feel about him not putting those images of violence into his head.

- Tell him he cannot attend slasher parties and that you will call the host parents to check on video selections.

- Offer to host video nights with acceptable movies which your child chooses.

- Use the "Ups and Downs with Feelings" board game to discuss the feelings you and he have about the movies. (See "Other Learning Materials Available.")

- Tell him that you protect him from violent attacks and that this *is* one. Don't let him go.

- Ask him if he has experienced violence.

Thanks to Gail Nordeman,
Suggestion Circle from Cincinnati, Ohio

Chapter 7

Building Self-Esteem

59. What can I do to encourage my children to be responsible for their own self-esteem?

- Hang a bulletin board in each of their rooms where they can post whatever is important to them. Mention what you see.

- Ask for positive messages for yourself. They will pick up how to do this from hearing you do it. If you keep your self-esteem high, they'll see how to do it.

- Teach them to separate helpful negative comments from destructive criticism and to keep only what's helpful.

- Encourage them to talk about their large and small triumphs.

- Be able to accept compliments yourself.

- Together, write down positive things about each child, and post the lists.

- Have their bedtime ritual include: "Four things I did well today are . . . "

- Teach them to ask for hugs when they want them.

- Play the "Ups and Downs with Feelings" game with them. (See "Other Learning Materials Available.")

- Don't force them to compete with the rest of the family. Let them be unique.

- Read them the affirmations for growth, and encourage them to ask for the ones they want each day. (See "Developmental Affirmations for All Ages.")

  (See also questions 29 and 65.)

  Thanks to Kathy Brinkerhoff,
  Suggestion Circle from Lafayette, California

60. My child sets himself up to be criticized. How can I help him?

- Ask yourself if this is the only way he gets attention from you and others.

- Watch the way he sets you up to criticize him. Point out his part in asking for criticism, and refuse to give the negative messages.

- Check to see if you are overly critical toward your son or yourself.

- Visualize him believing all the good stuff about himself, and visualize yourself as a nurturing and caring parent.

- Go ahead and give him lots of reinforcement that tells him you like him just the way he is.

- Tell him five things you like about him before he goes to bed each night.

- Be careful you don't give helpful messages in a critical voice.

- Read Clarke's *Self-Esteem: A Family Affair*. Learn about the four ways of parenting; then stick to giving him the positive nurturing and structuring messages. (See "Resources.")

- Catch him being good. Compliment him when you see him doing something the way you want him to.

  (See also questions 36, 45, and 59.)

Thanks to Toni Drucker, Suggestion Circle from Orinda, California

61. How do I as a parent help my child learn to reject negative messages and teasing at school?

- Don't accept negative messages yourself, and don't give them yourself.

- Read Clarke's *Self-Esteem: A Family Affair* to learn about the four ways of parenting, and give lots of positive messages at home. (See "Resources.")

- Teach the child specifically to ignore or to refuse to accept negative messages. Have him practice saying "I don't accept that" when he hears a negative message.

- Ask the teacher to work with the whole class on rejecting verbal abuse and teasing and on learning how to cope with both.

- Suggest to the principal that the whole school plan a self-esteem week.

- Affirm him. Say, "You are a worthwhile person. I love and respect you."

- Tell him that he doesn't have to believe the negative messages and that he can look for a kernel of truth in what people are telling him.

- Have him make a list of things he likes about himself. Invite everyone in the family to add to the list. Post it where he can see it every day.

- Teach him to throw hurtful stuff in the garbage can. You can do the same.

(See also questions 34, 36, and 60.)

Thanks to Deane Gradous,
Suggestion Circle from Wayzata, Minnesota

62. My eleven-year-old thinks that he knows everything. He won't take advice or instruction from anyone. What can I do?

- Provide him with some tougher challenges.

- Ask him to take charge of some family situations, and support his leadership role without giving advice. He will find out that there are some things he doesn't know.

- I have yet to meet an eleven-year-old who knows everything. Are you buying into this fiction in some way?

- Let him fail and take the full consequences of his failure without your interfering.

- As a responsible parent, you decide when to insist that things be done a certain way.

- When he is being successful, let him continue. Tell him to ask for help if he needs it.

- Give him affirmations for six- to twelve-year-olds like "You can find a way of doing things that works for you." (See "Affirmations for Growth—Structure.")

- Try saying "I feel . . . " or "For me it works to . . . " instead of being authoritarian and saying "Do it this way" or "You should do it this way."

- Let him do things away from home—Scouts, science center. Have him make his own arrangements. Give him opportunities to discover that things are not always as simple as they seem.

(See also question 15.)

Thanks to Linda Buranen,
Suggestion Circle from Plymouth, Minnesota

63. Our ten-year-old daughter puts herself down because she sees herself as overweight. Television feeds this image. How can we support her to accept herself as she is?

- Acknowledge that she thinks she is overweight. Assure her that you love her. Together, check with the doctor on an appropriate weight for her.

- Every day, give her positive messages *not* related to eating, food, body size, or appearance.

- Collect facts related to dieting. Be aware of problems related to food abuse, such as anorexia nervosa and bulimia.

- Health is a primary concern. How do you handle your own self-image and control your own weight?

- Give her the affirmations for Being. (See "Developmental Affirmations for All Ages.")

- Make sure that her eating is healthy and in control. Then shift the focus of your concern away from food issues.

- Check to see if she feels in control of other areas of her life (besides her weight).

- Suggest exercise to increase tone and energy. Take a fitness class together.

(See also question 66.)

Thanks to Gail Davenport,
Suggestion Circle from Edmonds, Washington

64. My child hits or scolds himself when he is frustrated or unable to handle a situation. What can I do to help him take better care of himself?

- People grow from their strengths. Emphasize his.

- Whenever you see him hurting himself, say "Stop that!" and then tell him you expect him to take care of himself.

- Say, "Don't hit yourself. I care about you."

- Ask, "What could you do instead of ragging on yourself?"

- Look for lots of ways to let him know you love him.

- Ask him, "Why do you think you should be able to handle *every* situation? Nobody else can."

- Let him see you handling your own frustrations without scolding yourself or others.

- Remind him of the house rule "We don't hurt people."

- Say, "If you feel like hitting yourself, try this fuss box instead." (See "The Fuss Box.")

  (See also questions 47 and 50.)

Thanks to Sue Hansen,
Suggestion Circle from Bellevue, Washington

65. My children don't believe they are responsible for how their days go. What can I say instead of "Have a good day"?

- How about "I love you! Build yourself a good day"?

- "I hope you accomplish a lot today."

- "Today is another challenge."

- "My love goes with you today. Make it a good one."

- "I wish you a wonderful day."

- Give them a kiss and a hug and tell them, "I hope you learn lots today."

- "Make today really special."

- "I'll be looking forward to hearing about your day when you get home."

- Saying "Make yourself a good day" encourages them to take responsibility for their day.

- "Learn something new today."

- "Smell the flowers."

- "Shalom."

- "Find something interesting today."

- Tuck a loving message in their pockets or lunch boxes.

- Invite them to "enjoy school."

- Read Kaufman and Raphael's *Stick Up for Yourself* with your children. (See "Resources.")

  (See also question 59.)

  Thanks to Sandra Sittko,
  Suggestion Circle from Saint Louis, Missouri

Chapter 8

Health and Wellness, Differences and Drugs

66. My eight-year-old daughter is overweight. What can I do or say to help her?

- Have a variety of fruit and vegetables around the house to satisfy her appetite after school.

- Buy stickers instead of food for treats.

- Catch her succeeding at eating correctly, and compliment her for that.

- Ask your daughter what help she wants from you.

- Take her to the grocery store so she can pick new foods that are healthy and low in fat.

- Ask her to check with herself whether she is eating for fun or out of boredom or because she's hungry and then to eat only when hungry.

- Find nutritional, low-calorie recipes, and try them together with her.

- Catch her succeeding, when she is substituting fun activities instead of eating.

- Give her lots of Being messages, and find time to be with her. (See "Developmental Affirmations for All Ages.")

- Make exercise a habit and a fun and enjoyable part of the daily routine.

- You have control over what you provide for eating in your house. Offer healthy, low-calorie food and snacks.

  (See also questions 16 and 63.)

  Thanks to Nat Houtz,
  Suggestion Circle from Lynwood, Washington

67. My son is eight years old and still wets the bed most nights. He can't go to sleepovers, and I'm tired of doing all the wash and smelling urine all the time. What can I do?

- Talk to your physician.
- Realize that bed-wetting is a problem of sleeping too deeply, and as his nervous system matures, he'll wake up to go.
- Have your son change his own sheets, put the sheets in the washing machine, and start it.
- Create a program of going to the bathroom at bedtime.
- Reassure him. Tell him that he is not the only boy his age to have this problem.
- See if your child wants an alarm to wake him up so he can go to the bathroom during the night. He has to manage it.
- Assure the child that you love him no matter what.
- Do not ever ridicule the child. You can tell him that *you* have a problem with the extra laundry.
- If your doctor says there is no organic reason, check for stress in your son's life. Child and family counselors are available to help.
- Remember Michael Landon did this, too.

Thanks to Kay Kubes,
Suggestion Circle from Saint Paul, Minnesota

68. My sixth-grade boy is short and a slow developer. The boys in physical education class keep bugging him. How can I help?

- Suggest that he talk to his P.E. teacher. Ask him if he wants you to be there, too.

- Ask for a conference with the school counselor.

- Remind the child to give himself time. He has a growth spurt coming up.

- Talk about neat men who happen to be short.

- Ask the doctor for a normal growth chart, and show him how wide the normal range is.

- Tell him about any men you know who developed late and are happy now.

- Have him take gymnastics, freestyle skiing, or soccer. Small boys have an advantage in those sports.

- Have him take karate or judo to learn to protect himself and to build self-confidence.

- Treat him according to his age, not his size.

Thanks to Gail Nordeman,
Suggestion Circle from Cincinnati, Ohio

69. My fifth-grade daughter has developed early. She wears a bra for comfort. The girls tease her, and the boys snap her bra straps. How can I help her?

- Tell her firmly and confidently that she is normal and that she is an early developer. She's OK. Others will catch up. Read Peter Mayle's *What's Happening to Me?* with her. (See "Resources.")

- Show her that each child can be different in some ways, such as tall or short, and can still be normal.

- Talk about how it was for you when you were a child so she does not feel alone.

- Say, "I love you the way you are, and your body is developing just the right way for you."

- Treat her like a fifth-grader, not older. Don't rush her to grow up to match her body.

- If your family physician is empathetic, ask for support from him or her.

- Teach her to evaluate teasing for what it says about the other person.

- Tell her that she is in charge of setting boundaries for her own body and that she can tell people when to *keep their hands off*.

- Go to school and tell the staff that the boys' behavior is not acceptable.

- Be sure that both mother and father affirm the daughter's changes.

(See also question 61.)

Thanks to Jean Clarke,
Suggestion Circle from Plymouth, Minnesota

70. My child has asthma, and although she looks like the other kids, this condition creates many problems, like missing school, low energy, and so on. How can I help?

- Tell your child she is wonderful, capable, and lovable. Give her lots of hugs!

- Look for stories or articles about people who have asthma and accomplish great things.

- Make certain her medical care is the best available for the problem.

- Learn all you can about asthma and its management, and teach this to her.
- Go to school and ask the school nurse to talk to the class about how kids need to manage their various medical problems, not just asthma.
- Make quiet activities meaningful and constructive.
- Tell her that it's OK to let other people know how she feels and what she needs.
- Teach her not to accept thoughtless, critical messages about her health.
- Acknowledge that she is different from other kids in some ways and the same in most ways.
- Regularly and often discuss the many ways in which she enjoys life.
- Expect her to manage her health, and support and help her while she learns how.
- Send her to a camp for asthmatic children.

(See also question 61.)

Thanks to Mary Kay Truitt,
Suggestion Circle from Saint Paul, Minnesota

71. How can I handle my son's reactions and sensitive feelings after being criticized by a boy in the neighborhood? My son has a repaired cleft lip.

- Tell him, "You look wonderful to *me!*"
- Train him to ignore such remarks and go on playing.
- Tell him to ignore this criticism and to stay away from that boy.
- Talk to the other boy's parents about the situation.

- Say, "I'm sorry he did that. He must not know much about cleft lips."

- Say, "Well, he could have been born with a cleft lip himself. Maybe he hasn't thought about that."

- Say, "I love all of you, and your lip is part of you."

- Say, "Wow! He hasn't learned very good manners yet, has he?"

- Suggest he say, "No big deal. Let's play."

(See also question 61.)

Thanks to Gail Davenport,
Suggestion Circle from Lynwood, Washington

72. The liquor in my cupboard is disappearing faster than I think it should. My twelve-year-old son's friends are in the house a lot; I'm afraid they're drinking it.

- Confront your son directly. Ask him about the situation. Decide with him how to handle it.

- Supervise play when his friends are in the house.

- Tell your son, "The liquor is going down faster than I'm using it. Adults use liquor, and children don't. You and your friends are *not* to take any of it."

- If his friends are drinking it, share your suspicions with their parents, and get their support in stopping the drinking.

- Lock the liquor cabinet.

- Teach him about the disease of alcoholism. Learn about it yourself, if you don't know.

- Tell him that alcohol is much more damaging to a growing liver than it is to a mature one. The damage could be life threatening and permanent.

(See also questions 56, 73, and 74.)

Thanks to Jean Clarke,
Suggestion Circle from Minneapolis, Minnesota

73. My eleven-year-old son wants to have a glass of wine with us at holiday dinners. Should we give it to him?

- Make a decision that is comfortable for you. Make sure he is clear about your decision.

- Alcohol is not appropriate for an eleven-year-old.

- Wait until the legal drinking age according to your state.

- Say no. Stick to it.

- Be clear about which traditional holidays and which children may have a glass of wine. Stick to it.

- With alcoholism a major problem in this country, why should anyone start drinking at eleven?

- If there is no alcoholism in your family, follow your family tradition. If there is, why have it at all?

- Provide an alternative, such as grape juice.

- Is wine necessary for anyone at this meal?

(See also questions 56, 72, and 74, and "Keeping School-Age Children Safe.")

Thanks to Sandra Sittko,
Suggestion Circle from Saint Paul, Minnesota

74. My friend called and said she had found marijuana in her boy's pocket. Her boy is my son's best friend.

- Thank her for telling you. Confront your son.

- Say to your son, "Your friend is in trouble. How can we help him? This is serious!"

- Don't get defensive. Ask your son if he and his friend have used marijuana and if he is ready to talk about it.

- After explaining to your son what you know, explain the legal risks of using marijuana and the consequences in your family.

- Take care not to take this casually or to act as if it is humorous.

- Explain the health hazards and consequences of marijuana use.

- Look to your own use of drugs, medications, and alcohol. Is there a need for change?

- Call the school and ask if they know of drug use or sources at school.

- Form a support group with other parents, and discuss this.

- Encourage the school to incorporate a drug abuse prevention program.

- Tell your son how important he is to you and how concerned you are.

- Contact the National Clearinghouse for Drug Abuse Information. (See "Resources.")

(See also questions 56, 72, and 73.)

Thanks to Christine Ternand,
Suggestion Circle from Minneapolis, Minnesota

75. How do I talk to my child about sex and AIDS?

- Find out what your child is being taught at school.

- Ask your child to tell you how AIDS can be prevented.

- Keep the topic open; don't let it become taboo.

- Say, "Most people who get the AIDS virus don't get symptoms for many years. But AIDS is deadly and must be taken very, very seriously."

- Be sure to discuss the dangers of handling used condoms and discarded hypodermic needles that may contain the AIDS virus.

- Tell your child that AIDS is not only a gay person's disease; it is spread by sexual encounters and dirty needles.

- Talk straight. Talk about both the facts and about your feelings and values about sex. Find out what she knows and feels and what she thinks this means for her life.

- Buy the *What's Happening to My Body?* books for girls and boys, by Madaras and Madaras and by Madaras and Saavedra. (See "Resources.") Read them with your children once you feel they are old enough to understand.

- Any biology teacher can discuss the mechanics of sex. *You* talk about the important stuff: cherishing another human being, loving touch, commitment, and all that.

- Don't neglect the spiritual aspect of intimacy.

- Volunteer to work for a local women's assault group if that will make it easier for you to talk about sex and AIDS.

  (See also "Safer Sex.")

Thanks to Sara Monser,
Suggestion Circle from Lafayette, California

Chapter 9

The Job of the Parent

76. It seems to me that my older children are taking over my role as parent with the younger children. What shall I do?

- Describe to them what they are doing, and then intervene and tell them that you are in charge.

- To some extent this is normal. They are learning and practicing being responsible. However, be sure to set limits. For example, discipline and final decisions are up to the parents.

- Discuss with the children your responsibilities and theirs. Thank them for their assistance in taking care of themselves and one another.

- Ask yourself, Have I given up my parenting role? Am I afraid to have them grow up and gain responsibility? Is what they are doing actually OK?

- Say, "I am the parent."

- Ask them to switch roles with you for twenty minutes and to take care of you instead of bossing the little kids.

- Give them lots of nurturing, and reward the positive parenting skills you see them developing.

- Tell them you love them and appreciate their good parenting skills. Remind them that you are responsible for being the parent.

Thanks to Deane Gradous,
Suggestion Circle from Wayzata, Minnesota

77. What are some ways an adult can be respectful to children in order to set an example for them?

- Give them privacy.

- Don't talk down to them. Talk at eye level.

- Show courtesy, respect, and empathy for them, and expect them to give you the same.

- Share rule setting.

- Listen to what they have to say. Ask about events and problems that are important to them. Ask their opinions.

- Keep your promises, and follow through on rules.

- Compliment them on things they do well, and tell them how much you love them.

- Respect others and yourself. Be honest. Be kind and understanding. Explain your actions and feelings.

- Introduce them by name to friends and acquaintances.

- Admit your mistakes, and apologize when you are wrong.

- Say "please" and "thank you."

- Every time I switch roles with my son for a few minutes, we both learn oodles about being more respectful to each other.

- Tell the kids what to expect.

• Only have secrets that are fun for all of you.

> *Thanks to Suzanne Morgan,*
> *Suggestion Circle from Albert Lea, Minnesota*

78. How can I avoid power struggles with my ten-year-old son? He hassles me and yells a lot.

• Bring his behavior to his attention, and tell him how you feel about it.

• Assess what he is trying to tell you with his behavior. Is he in competition with you? For what?

• Change *your* behavior for one week. Refuse to push or nag. Observe the results.

• Reward any signs of cooperation.

• Check with other parents to see if his behavior is in the range of normal.

• Limit yourself to giving him three suggestions a day. Ask him to try out one suggestion. Reward him when he changes his behavior.

• Double the number of hugs that you give him.

• Spend time playing with him.

• Refuse to negotiate nonnegotiable rules.

• Hassle with him in a loving way when you feel good. If you don't know how to hassle, you can find out in *Self-Esteem: A Family Affair*, by Jean Illsley Clarke. (See "Resources.")

• Kids this age need to hassle about rules. You might think about how much hassling you are willing to do on any given day.

- Ask him to yell in other places, like in the closet or shower. (See also question 25.)

Thanks to Sandra Sittko,
Suggestion Circle from Saint Louis, Missouri

79. How can I as a parent stay peaceful in the midst of my child's complaining, hassling, and put-downs?

- Have the child write or draw her complaints for you to see.

- When she starts, wear earplugs; when she stops take them out, and tell her to ask for what she wants directly.

- Sing.

- Let her know that her put-downs bother you and that she must speak respectfully.

- Think about what you want to express other than irritation, and then do it. Try affirmations instead of yelling.

- Practice centering with her. Refer to *The Centering Book*, by Hendricks and Wills. (See "Resources.")

- Make a "no put-down" rule for the entire family, and enforce it.

- Visualize your family cooperating in a loving, fun way.

- Take better care of yourself; spend time alone; get the rest and exercise you need.

- Avoid complaining and hassling yourself for a while. (See also question 77.)

Thanks to Ellen Peterson,
Suggestion Circle from Lafayette, California

80. My child often doesn't tell me about things that happen to him. How can I get him to tell me? I think parents should know what is going on.

- Model trust by sharing things with your spouse in front of the child.

- Set aside five to ten minutes a day with the child, and invite him to talk about anything he wants to talk about. Affirm him for talking to you.

- Be trustworthy. Don't betray his confidences.

- When he does talk, be sure not to interrupt or ridicule.

- Let's face it. Our children will never tell us everything. However, if you have a trusting relationship, the important things will come out.

- Talk to your kids about your life.

- Rhea Zakich's *The Ungame* really gets everyone talking and sharing. It is not competitive in any way and is very non-threatening. (See "Resources.")

- Ask him about what has been happening in his life. If he chooses not to share anything with you, show him you love him, and tell him you will ask again because you care about him.

- Use active listening techniques. Read Thomas Gordon's *Parent Effectiveness Training*. (See "Resources.")

(See also question 77.)

Thanks to Sandra Sittko,
Suggestion Circle from Saint Paul, Minnesota

81. I discussed my child's problem with my doctor, and I just don't feel comfortable with what she says we should do. What do I do now?

- Consult another physician.

- Discuss your concerns with family and friends, and ask what they would do.
- If the doctor is a good listener, state your concerns to her.
- If this is not life threatening, try what you have been told by your physician. It may work.
- Trust your intuition.
- Check to see if you heard right.
- Ask a nurse with whom you feel comfortable what she thinks of your concern.
- If the problem is urgent, do something. Don't stay in indecision.
- Realize that doctors are people, too. They don't have all the answers.
- Look up information on the problem at the library, and see if her treatment plan corresponds with recent material on the subject.
- Ask your doctor if there are other medical viewpoints on the problem.
- Trust your feelings about the doctor. If you trust her, try what she suggests; if not, find someone you do trust.

Thanks to Kay Kubes,
Suggestion Circle from Saint Paul, Minnesota

82. My in-laws interfere by hinting that my kids shouldn't have to follow family rules. How can I deal with them when we are face to face?

- Be your own person. Say, "At our house, parents make the rules, and the children must follow them."
- Let them know that your family has decided on rules for living together.

- Say, "We expect our children to follow our family rules. Do not encourage the children to break rules."

- Ask, "Will you help me by reinforcing the family rules when I am not here?" (If they decline, find ways to shorten the visits.)

- Post a few of the family rules on the refrigerator. Point them out to your in-laws.

- Ask your spouse to tell them to "turn it off."

- Notice things they do well with the children, and compliment them.

- Rethink your rules. Maybe you will decide that your in-laws are right about some of them.

- When they drop hints, clap your hands over your ears and say, "I hope the children didn't hear that."

(See also question 17.)

Thanks to Carole Gesme,
Suggestion Circle from Minnetonka, Minnesota

83. My in-laws criticize me and the children. I want to stop this, but I don't want to alienate them. Do you have any suggestions?

- Tell them you love and appreciate their interest but that their messages may be damaging to your children.

- When they criticize, tell them in a matter-of-fact tone, "Criticism hurts. I want you to tell her when she does well."

- Next time you are with them, give two positive messages to each person there, including yourself and your child. Stay busy doing that.

- Trust your feelings to know what to do. You may need to tell your family how you feel.

- Teach your child how to reject unhelpful or negative messages. Compliment her about how well she does that.

- Read *Ouch, That Hurts!*, by Jean Illsley Clarke, and use the parts that will help you and your child. (See "Resources.")

- Ask them to be kind instead of critical.

- Tell them you are learning how to be directive without being critical, and you want them to practice with you.

- When they send a zapper to you, say, "Ouch," or fall down on the floor and say, "I'm wounded."

- Have your children wear buttons or T-shirts that say, "Be gentle. Human being inside."

(See also question 21.)

Thanks to Pearl Noreen,
Suggestion Circle from Seattle, Washington

84. My spouse and I are getting a divorce. I'm upset about it. How can I help the kids?

- Get help for yourself first. Go to a support group or counselor.

- Tell your kids that you and your spouse are getting a divorce because you two can no longer live together and that it is *not* their fault.

- Tell the truth. Don't make it worse or better than it really is.

- Answer the children's questions directly.

- Think how to get support for the kids. Now's the time to turn to grandparents, aunts, uncles, and friends.

- Spend extra time with the kids when you are feeling good.

- Find out if there is a support group at school for kids whose parents are going through a divorce.

- See *The Kids' Book of Divorce*, by Eric Rofes. If you and your spouse are fighting, get *Something Is Wrong at My House,* by Diane Davis. (See "Resources.")

- Tell them, "Because we can't live together doesn't mean we will love you any less."

- Get each child a copy of Heegaard's *When Mom and Dad Separate* for them to draw in. (See "Resources.")

- Be certain that any anger toward your spouse is not directed at or through your kids.

Thanks to Sandra Sittko,
Suggestion Circle from Saint Louis, Missouri

85. My stepson resents my being in charge of him. He ignores me and is negative toward me. What can I do?

- Offer him unconditional love without expecting him to return the same to you.

- Say to him, "What you need is important to me," and "I'm glad I know you." (See "Developmental Affirmations for All Ages.")

- Affirm yourself as a worthwhile person. Don't take his attacks personally. Require him to abide by the established family rules.

- Consistent, skillful parenting pays off in establishing a bond with a child who did not ask you to be his stepmother. Keep at it, not at him.

- Expect your spouse to help insist that your stepson follow rules while he is with you.

- Let him know you are not afraid of his anger.

- Remember that building your relationship with him will take time. Get support from others during this period.

- Consider how he is feeling about the situation. Encourage him to talk about how he is feeling.

- Be careful that each of you has private space and time.

- Visualize the family as you want it to be in two years.

Thanks to Nat Houtz,
Suggestion Circle from Lynwood, Washington

86. I have to go to work. How can I find good before- and after-school care for my child?

- Chat with mothers in the neighborhood or apartment building; find out who they use and what they look for in a caregiver.

- Look for a neighbor with children about the same age who might care for your child.

- Check with the schools for latchkey programs.

- Call churches to see if they have lists of qualified sitters.

- Call your county welfare agency for the names of licensed day-care providers. Interview several providers before deciding.

- Ask a neighbor who is at home with an infant if he or she would welcome an older child twice a day.

- Put an ad in the church bulletin or other local publication.

- Get references. Trust your feelings about the setting that will be best for your child.

Thanks to Roxanne Michelson,
Suggestion Circle from Saint Paul, Minnesota

87. I'm beginning to resent that I am doing too much for the rest of the family, but they expect me to. How can I change that?

- Compliment them when someone in the family does something for you.

- Establish a specific amount of time just for yourself every day.

- Have a family meeting; present your problem and ask for suggestions.

- Look at your expectations to see if they are reasonable. For example, don't get white carpets if you have four kids under twelve.

- Teach others how to do chores. Teach one chore at a time.

- If it is someone else's job, leave it undone.

- Put a notice on the refrigerator:

  Dear Children,
  I have changed. Please notice that I no longer _____.
  Please compliment me when I _____.

- Remember, kids don't have to like doing chores; they just have to do them.

- Assign chores to each child. Make a book of chore coupons for each, and allow each child once a week to give you the coupon and have you do the chore for him or her as a special favor. This will teach children that your help is a gift, not a right.

Thanks to Betty Beach,
Suggestion Circle from Minnetonka Beach, Minnesota

88. How do I get my kids to respect my right to have some time alone with my friends or on the phone?

- Say, "We'll have time together when I'm done." Follow through on your promise, and spend time with them when you are off the phone or when the guests are gone.

- Be firm and fair. If they disrupt a phone call, tell them, "This is my time. Your time was earlier or will come later. Don't interrupt me again. I respect your time, and I expect you to respect my time."

- Negotiate rules and guidelines to be followed by everyone in the family. Tell them that you need time separate from them and that they are also entitled to privacy.

- Keep a timer by the phone so that you keep your phone calls the length you want.

- Set aside one hour a day when you are to be left alone. I know a mom with eight kids who does it, so I know it can work.

- Tell them what you think and what they are to do while you are on the phone, such as "When I have friends over, you are to give me thirty minutes of uninterrupted time. Let me know if you are hurt or in trouble; otherwise, play by yourselves."

- Respect their rights, and expect them to respect yours. Set consequences for the times when they don't.

Thanks to Ellen Peterson,
Suggestion Circle from Walnut Creek, California

89. My neighbors were talking about molesting and incest. I wonder if this could be the root of my daughter's behavior problems. I'm scared about this.

- You can think about this and not let your fear stop your thinking. You can talk to a counselor or doctor.

- Tell your daughter you expect her to trust her feelings and to tell you if anything doesn't feel right.

- Talk to her gently and nurturingly.

- Ask your daughter to draw a picture of your family; then you look for what the picture says about her place in the family.

- Teach her that harmful secrets are not OK. Only problems that are known can be solved.

- Talk to your doctor.

- Talk to a counselor or someone at your local child protection service about your fears.

- Believe that your daughter is telling you something with her behavior. Stick with it until you find out what it is. If not incest, it is something else.

- Read *No More Secrets for Me,* by Oralee Wachter, with your daughter. Read *No More Secrets,* by Caren Adams and Jennifer Fay, for lots of specific things you can do. Newman's *Never Say Yes to a Stranger* is also helpful. (See "Resources.")

Thanks to Mary Kay Truitt,
Suggestion Circle from Saint Paul, Minnesota

90. How can I handle my anger with my child?

- Talk to someone you trust.

- Keep an anger journal. Write down your feelings.

- Don't yell. Focus on solving the problem. Come back to the subject.

- Listen and ask the child, "What do you need?"

- Take a walk.

- Think! Figure out what will help resolve the problem. Then do it.

- Remember three great things about your child to help you put your anger in perspective.

- Give responsibility for the problem to the child if he is behaving badly.

- Delete expletives.

- Affirm yourself. Say "I am a lovable and loving person" ten times.

- Remember, your worth as a person is separate from what your child does.

- Get a cup of coffee or tea, and collect your thoughts and emotions.

- Own your feelings. Use "I" statements.

- Use the fuss box. (See "The Fuss Box.")

- Stop and think.

- Learn about child development to see if you are expecting too much. (See "Ages and Stages" and "Common Pitfalls.")

- Read Lerner's *Dance of Anger*. (See "Resources.")

    (See also question 10.)

Thanks to Harold Nordeman,
Suggestion Circle from Cincinnati, Ohio

91. While my seven-year-old daughter was being cared for by a seventeen-year-old neighbor girl, the neighbor girl went with her mother to get her hair cut and left my daughter with the father and sixteen-year-old brother. The brother and my daughter went up to the boy's bedroom. While they were there, my daughter told me, the boy told her to put her hand on him. She did and said, "That's your penis!" He said, "No, it's not; it's a picture frame." She said, "That's your penis," and went downstairs. I told my daughter she'd done well. What shall I do?

- Do not allow this girl to baby-sit for your child again on the chance that abuse from one family member may be an indication of abuse by other family members.

- Call your local child protection service.

- Address the boy directly. If he denies it and will not accept responsibility, then his parents should be responsible to get help for him.

- Write down all the messages you have in your mind about a situation like this. Pick out the ones that are helpful, and act on them.

- Confront the boy.

- Remember, if you don't confront the boy, other children may be victimized.

- In front of his parents, tell the boy his behavior is totally unacceptable.

Thanks to Bobbi Mlekodaj,
Suggestion Circle from Minneapolis, Minnesota

Moving On to the Teenage Years

People who live in cold climates like to tell—and retell—an old joke about their unpredictable weather. It goes something like this: if you don't like the weather, just wait ten minutes.

Well, living with a teenager is often like living in a northern clime. While teens can be wonderfully engaging, they are anything but predictable. One minute bristling and stormy, the next minute they are warm, companionable, and funny. For parents of teens, walking the tightrope between the two extremes constitutes both a reward and a challenge.

When dealing with your teenagers, keep in mind that just like two- or four-year-olds, your children are not necessarily out to get you with their behavior. In fact, at their most trying, they may be doing exactly what they are supposed to do. They are striving to separate from their parents and establish their own personal identity. They are also seeking boundaries and assistance in their bid for independence, and your responses to their growing can help or hinder them in this process.

What do you need to know as your children enter the teen years?

First of all, keep in mind the stage they have just completed. As six- to twelve-year-olds, your children learned to establish rules and structure, and they developed and practiced using new skills.

Teenagers need to develop a sense of personal identity, explore their sexuality, and continue to separate from their parents.

Your task is to support them in this process, strive to keep the lines of communication open, affirm their developing bodies, and keep in mind their need for privacy.

While you cannot and should not prevent teens from exploring their world, you can provide a degree of preventive safety. Remember that parents sometimes need to protect teenagers from themselves.

Set appropriate boundaries, and establish a realistic structure. Be clear about which rules must be followed and which ones can be negotiated. Follow through with predetermined consequences.

Most important, stay with the parenting process. At times you may be tempted to abdicate your job as a parent. If your relationship with your growing child seems like an adult friendship, that's a preview of what's to come. But while they are teenagers, your children do not need you to be a "buddy." They do need a responsible parent who offers love and constancy and who remains actively involved in helping them to grow into competent and independent adults.

Rick Bell, Ph.D., and Lonnie Bell, editor/writer

Coauthors of a forthcoming book based on Rick's fourteen years of work with fathers

2

Help!
For Parents of Teenagers

Ages and Stages

If you sometimes feel as though much of your teen's energy is directed toward pulling away from the family, you're probably right. Teenagers' process of separating includes their deciding on a unique personal identity and determining what values are their own, what works in their relationships with others, and who will care about them besides their families. In addition, teens must decide where their growing sexuality fits in with each earlier developmental task and then figure out how they, as newly separated persons, will fit into the adult world.

Although teens may loudly proclaim otherwise, they have not left childhood behind. Rather, they are recycling earlier developmental tasks (see the sections on recycling) with the added dimension of sexuality.

The exact ages at which individuals recycle each stage may vary from the descriptions that follow. Every teen has her own timetable for development, but the sequence of development will flow for most teens approximately as described. Expect the process to include frequent returns to earlier stages as your teen completes leftover bits and pieces of an earlier task.

- At age thirteen, the familiar childhood body disappears, and the new body of the early adolescent emerges. The person inside this changing body requires the assurance of *nurturing*, much as a newborn does. Your thirteen-year-old may ask for special foods, rides to school, new clothes, and infinite patience. She will often check out whether she is still loved and lovable as she begins to take on the shape of an adult sexual being. Lots of nonsexual touching and parental hugs along with continued attention, support, and understanding will help her know that her growing up is wonderful and that she is not to use sex to get her touching needs met.

- By late thirteen, if your teen has come to trust that you will accept and nurture her as she continues to grow, she'll be free to *explore* new experiences—sports, jobs, friends—with energy and enthusiasm. Sometimes these explorations appear to lack direction, but they provide your teen with important experience and new information about her own talents, interests, and relationships to others, which she then uses in creating her own separate and unique identity.

- At fourteen, all these new experiences and feelings must soon be integrated into the old beliefs and values that your child internalized during her growing up. Your fourteen-year-old may seem forgetful and daydreamy, resistant and negative, charming and compliant. These confusing and contrary behaviors are the visible signs of your child's growing desire to *think for herself*.

- By age fifteen, your teen has internalized rules about *power* in relation to others, including and perhaps especially rules about power in relating to the opposite sex. Challenging the rules and values of family, friends, and society helps her examine and update her own rules and values. If the adults in her life can support her exploring without feeling unduly resistant, threatened, or rejected, they may find a sixteen-year-old who is a source of pleasure and friendly stimulation. Adults who respect and support a teen's exploration toward individuality will help her learn to be direct in expressing her needs. She won't have to resort to manipulation or to using her sexuality to get what she needs.

- The middle or late adolescent, using both adults and peers as models, "tries on" different attitudes, rules, ways of thinking, talking, and relating as she reworks old assumptions and feelings about who she is in light of all her new experiences and sexuality.

- Around age seventeen, teens moving into competent adulthood are practicing *responsibility* in getting their needs met, in thinking and expressing their own thoughts and opinions, in recognizing their own feelings, and in preparing to leave home to become separate adults in a grown-up world.

What can parents do to help? When we show teens that we feel OK about not having all the answers, we help our children know that they can figure out answers for themselves. For example, discovering that we've been using a rule that isn't helpful and choosing to change that rule validates our children in their search for rules that they can make their own. It's important to ask our growing-up children for hugs; that teaches them how to get the touching they need and that it's OK to ask for hugs; it also reminds them that everyone needs nurturing touch—that is, touch that has nothing to do with sex. When, as parents, we enjoy being a man or a woman, we assure our teens that it's satisfying to grow from being a boy to a man or a girl to a woman. To help teens know that positive relationships include disagreements and problem solving as well as joy, we let them witness parents arguing and resolving their differences.

Our children in their teen years will be building on the skills they acquired throughout the years before. As they recycle the developmental stages of those earlier years, they have many opportunities to expand, rework, and make important decisions about what they've learned, about who they are, and about how to become responsible, independent adults.

Parents can use all of the affirmations listed in "Developmental Affirmations for All Ages" to guide them as they offer supportive messages for teenage developmental tasks and for earlier tasks that are recycled during adolescence.

Sara Monser

Affirmations for Growth—Identity, Sexuality, and Separation

Affirmations are all the things we do or say that imply that our children are lovable and capable. Belief in these affirmations supports teenagers in their self-acceptance, their ability to take responsibility for themselves, and their independence, and it sets the stage for adult developmental tasks.

Here are some special affirming messages that will help young people during their adolescent stage of growth. You give these affirmations by the way you

- Interact with your adolescent
- Respond to his sometimes dramatic changes in mood and interests as he swings from recycling one stage to another
- Admire his emerging sexuality without being seductive
- Support his emotional separation first
- Support his physical separation later or support his growing independence while he continues to live at home
- Say these affirmations directly in a supportive, loving way.

Of course, you have to believe the messages yourself, or they come off as confusing or crazy double messages. If you don't understand or believe an affirmation, don't give that one until you do believe it.

Affirmations for Identity, Sexuality, and Separation

- You can know who you are and learn and practice skills for independence.
- You can learn the difference between sex and nurturing and be responsible for your needs and behavior.
- You can develop your own interests, relationships, and causes.
- You can learn to use old skills in new ways.
- You can grow in your maleness or femaleness and still be dependent at times.
- I look forward to knowing you as an adult.
- My love is always with you, and I trust you to ask for my support.

Once human beings enter a certain developmental stage, they need the affirmations from that stage for the rest of their lives, so teenagers continue to need the affirmations from the earlier stages. You can offer the affirmations singly or in groups whenever they seem appropriate.

The affirmations for Being, for Exploring and Doing, for Thinking, for Identity and Power, and for Structure are all listed in the section entitled "Developmental Affirmations for All Ages."

Teenagers who didn't decide to believe these affirmations at younger ages have a wonderful chance to incorporate them during adolescence. If something happened in their lives or in the family that interfered with a decision to believe them, or if you, the parent, didn't understand the importance of the developmental tasks, act now. Remember, it is never too late for you to start believing and offering the affirmations.

You can learn more about how to use these affirmations in

families by reading Clarke's *Self-Esteem: A Family Affair* or Clarke and Dawson's *Growing Up Again*. (See "Resources.") When you discover additional affirmations that your adolescent needs, write them down and give them to your teenager.

The Editors

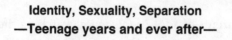

Identity, Sexuality, Separation
—Teenage years and ever after—

You can know who you are and learn and practice skills for independence.

You can learn the difference between sex and nurturing and be responsible for your needs and behavior.

You can develop your own interests, relationships and causes.

You can learn to use old skills in new ways.

You can grow in your maleness or femaleness and still be dependent at times.

I look forward to knowing you as an adult.

My love is always with you. I trust you to ask for my support.

Copy these ovals and color them dark blue.
Post them for daily reading.

Parents of Teenagers Get Another Chance—Recycling

Some parents of adolescents enjoy watching the emerging adult as she unfolds, and they enjoy "letting go," but others resist the separation and try to maintain control. Almost all parents find the daily demands of nurturing, challenging, and setting limits for adolescents taxing at times. Whatever parents feel when children go through the transition from childhood to adulthood, one of the benefits of this period is that it triggers parents themselves to recycle or to continue working on their own tasks of becoming whole, separate human beings, of owning their sexuality, and of expanding their concept of their place in the larger world. Reexamining our own needs for nurturing, exploring, deciding who we are, and what rules we live by can parallel these stages in our adolescents. Parents who "recycle" and recreate better ways to do old tasks along with their kids may make the journey through the teen years a satisfying adventure.

Affirmations for Growth

The affirmations that are helpful to our children are also healthy for us. (See "Developmental Affirmations for All Ages.") If we didn't get the affirmations we needed the first time around (and many of us didn't), we can think how they fit for us, and accept them now as we offer them to our children. (See also "Parents Get Another Chance—Recycling.")

Jean Illsley Clarke

Common Pitfalls

Sometimes, as adolescents go about their developmental tasks, they do things that are misinterpreted by parents, who may then be overly severe or hurtful in an attempt to stop or control these normal behaviors. Parents may believe that they are "disciplining," but when they punish their teenagers for doing what is developmentally correct and normal or when parents back off from setting rules and standards, teens are hurt physically or emotionally.

The following behaviors of young people this age are frequently misunderstood:

- Teens are beginning to experiment with ways of *expressing their budding sexuality.* They have many sexual behaviors and attitudes to explore and decisions to make before they are ready for sexual intercourse. It is neglectful for adults not to set guidelines for appropriate adolescent behavior. Unfortunately, many media in our society are reinforcing the fantasy that these children are highly desirable sexual objects. In spite of physical signs of sexual maturity, teens still need the protection of caring adults. It is always sexual abuse when someone misuses a *trust* relationship and gives suggestive kisses or touches a child sexually in any way. The adult is responsible: an adolescent is *never* responsible for the seduction. If there is a difference of more than three years of age between participants, and one participant is a minor, sexual touching is considered rape by law in many states.

- One of the most important tasks of the teenager is to *separate* from the family and become an independent adult. (See "Ages and Stages" and "Four Ways Young People Separate.") Many times, teens will escalate negative behaviors as part of this separating task. Caring adults who don't understand this need for separation may become verbally or physically abusive or may back off, instead of calmly continuing to set and enforce the important limits.

- As part of the maturing process, teens rework and *upgrade earlier developmental tasks.* (See "Ages and Stages" and "Affirmations for Growth—Identity, Sexuality, and Separation.") The emotional ups and downs that accompany these recycling activities may appear confusing if they are not seen as part of normal development. Some adults may become abusive in response to their feelings of confusion.

- Teenagers are making early decisions about life choices, including future schooling, careers, and life goals. Adults need to support teens in sorting out what they truly seek, rather than expecting the young people to fulfill some of the parents' unmet dreams.

Christine Ternand, M.D.

Keeping Adolescents Safe

It is easy to believe that teens are "old enough to take care of themselves," but parents are still responsible for their teen's safety. To protect teens, parents do the following:

- Attend to all of the safety issues from the earlier stage (see "Keeping School-Age Children Safe"), and overcome any reluctance to offer direct information about AIDS and pregnancy.

- Remember that teens need some clear rules—for example, about curfews and car privileges—and that they need to have these rules enforced.

- Make certain teens are capable of staying alone before leaving them alone. Pay special attention to their ability to follow social and safety rules.

- Give them permission to say no to peer pressure.

- Give them permission to call home *anytime* they need help or to take a taxi if it's needed for their safety.

- Teach safe driving skills in a positive, respectful way. Monitor their driving until they have developed skillful, careful driving habits.

- Become aware of the extent of alcohol abuse and drug abuse in the teens' environment, and take action to help them protect themselves from that abuse.

- Continue to be a reliable source of information about people and the world. Explain about sexual maturity, safety, and responsibility to teenagers caringly, lovingly, and knowledgeably, or get a specially trained adult to do it. Information from other sources, such as peers or washroom walls, is often inaccurate or incomplete. In addition, parents supply teens with accurate printed information about these topics.

- Help teens establish a sense of personal responsibility, but do not exploit them by expecting them to take major responsibility for the household or for child care, both of which are functions of the parents. Do not allow sports coaches or teachers to exploit them either.

Christine Ternand, M.D.

Structuring for Responsibility and Independence

An adequate internal structure is the foundation for independence and responsibility. *All the ways people arrange and organize their thinking, feeling, and behavioral responses make up this structure.* Preteens have developed their structure by gathering information, developing skills, and forming attitudes and beliefs about themselves, others, and the world. Some of these attitudes, conclusions, and beliefs were formed when the children were too young to understand fully what they were choosing.

During adolescence, children are faced with a variety of decisions and are offered many opportunities to update their early attitudes, conclusions, and beliefs in order to support their growing maturity. This process often creates both internal and external conflict. One of the ways in which parents help their teens to become responsible and independent is by encouraging them to amend or update earlier structures.

Responsibility is a learned skill. Teens do not learn to be responsible and independent all at once; rather, they learn to take over and accomplish the tasks of self-care gradually by practicing many skills and by learning through failures and successes. Parents need to encourage teens to make their own choices in safe areas. There are many nonharmful areas—such as dress, hairstyle, and music—in which teens can develop their separate identity. If parents attempt to control their teens' behavior in all areas (especially those that are safe for teenagers but not necessarily comfortable for the parents), then teens may resort to more harmful activities such as drugs and inappropriate sexual behavior in order to establish themselves as separate from their parents.

Remember, there are many "right" ways to parent teenagers. Keeping in mind that each family is different and each adolescent is unique, you can use the following guidelines, as well as those already mentioned, to create the type of environment that fosters responsibility and independence:

- Visualize your teen as competent and lovable.

- Listen to the thoughts, content, and emotional level of your teen's communication in a nonjudgmental way.

- Challenge through direct communication any beliefs and attitudes your teenager holds that you believe are destructive.

- Recognize, praise, and affirm all positive behaviors and attitudes. Continue to give unconditional love, and support the development of values and morals in all areas.

- Continue to set healthy limits in areas that are potentially dangerous. Limits provide a sense of security as teens practice different ways of being independent.

- Praise what your teen does well, while holding him accountable for what he does poorly. Allow him to experience the consequences, negative or positive, of his behavior.

- Encourage teens to make responsible moral decisions about the expression of their maturing sexuality, as well as about other areas.

- Give permission to and expect your teen to identify and reject destructive messages that invite diminished self-esteem or that do not help him to be a responsible person.

- Support teens as they seek solutions to problems.

Helping adolescents learn structures for independence and responsibility is a very important gift that parents can give their children. When it seems to parents that they are putting more energy into the parent-teen relationship than the kids are, this is probably true. Think back to your own teenage years, and recall the most important thing about any year of your adolescence. Chances are, it was *not* "getting along well with my parents." The children are doing their job, which is to separate. You do yours, which is to continue to provide love, support, and a flexible structure as you separate from them.

Gail Nordeman

Chapter 10

School

92. My teenager is failing a class. He is not concerned, but I am. What can I do?

- This child may need to fail and take the consequences to get the message that he is responsible for his schoolwork.

- Find out why he is not interested. Ask him to think of ways he can make the course interesting for himself.

- Arrange a meeting with the teacher for your son and you.

- Ask him what he plans to do about it.

- Check to see if this is solely his problem or if it is part of a larger family problem, such as grief, divorce, or alcoholism.

- Give him a choice. Take a privilege away if he doesn't raise his grade. Decide on a reward for improvement.

- Consider moving him to a teacher or school that will expect more of him or be more suited to his needs.

- Give him lots of recognition for who he is aside from this problem.

- Remember your worth is not determined by his grades.

- Have his hearing tested. Some children who can't hear pretend they don't care about grades.

(See also questions 100, 141, 148, 152, and "Structuring for Responsibility and Independence.")

Thanks to Suzanne Morgan,
Suggestion Circle from Albert Lea, Minnesota

93. My fifteen-year-old daughter came home with two D's and four C's. She is capable of B's and wants to go to college. How do I encourage her to believe in herself and to improve her grades?

- Let her know you will always love her and that grades are for her, not you.

- Brainstorm with her ways she can bring her grades up and how you can help if she needs it.

- Be available to listen.

- Celebrate each grade she improves.

- Be sure women have permission and encouragement to be smart in your family, even if that means she is smarter than her boyfriend.

- If poor grades are a part of a bigger problem, like depression, ask her to go with you to a school counselor. Be sure she knows what grade point average she needs to get into college.

- Help her make a study schedule, if she wants your help. Eliminate distractions—radio, TV, phone calls, and so on, during study times.

- Get a tutor for her.

- Check on drugs and sexual activity. Confront her if you find a problem.

- Help her develop a peer study group.

- Ask her if her friends are supporting her wish to go to college. She may need some new friends.

(See also question 147, "Ages and Stages," and "Affirmations for Growth—Identity, Sexuality, and Separation.")

Thanks to Roxy Chuchna,
Suggestion Circle from Albert Lea, Minnesota

94. Our daughter will not get involved in school activities. What can I do?

- Provide opportunities for her to join other groups besides those at school—for example, the Y, civic center groups, church or synagogue groups, hospital volunteers, search-and-rescue teams, and so on.
- Trust her to know what is best for her.
- Invite her to bring her friends to the house. Casually ask about their school activities. Find out how their parents view their activities.
- Look at the possibility that some children are not interested in school activities and still do just fine in the business world and adult life.
- Check out your motives. Let her be who she is. Give her the freedom to be herself.
- Go to some mother-daughter or father-daughter events with her.
- Look at her friends. What are their interests?
- Explain how school activities will benefit her in the future—job résumé, college applications, and so on.
- Is she in some other group activities? If not, tell her you want her to find one activity, in or out of school, to participate in.

• If the girl is a real loner, consider some counseling.

(See also "Affirmations for Growth—Identity, Sexuality, and Separation.")

Thanks to Nat Houtz,
Suggestion Circle from Seattle, Washington

95. My athletic child is being pushed by his coach to do and achieve more and more at sports. I'm not sure what to do, if anything.

• Look at whether sports are interfering with his growth as a well-rounded person. If so, decide with him how to achieve a healthy balance.

• There are limits on this. You and your son decide what they are. Limit the coach if you have to.

• Be aware that coaches can sometimes influence even academic grades in order to keep an athlete playing. This teaches manipulation and dishonesty while cheating a student of a sound education.

• Discuss with your child the degree to which he minds being pushed and what he would like you to do to help him out.

• Watch carefully that he doesn't hide injuries from you in order to keep on playing.

• During this time, give lots of strokes for Being: "I love you whether you play or not."

• Discuss the pros and cons of playing a sport with your child. Allow him to make his own decision, and support him.

• Ask your son, "Are your sports fun? Do *you* like playing?"

(See also "Ages and Stages" and "Affirmations for Growth —Identity, Sexuality, and Separation.")

Thanks to Sara Monser,
Suggestion Circle from Lafayette, California

96. One teacher at school is giving my daughter a hard time. What do I do about it?

- Set up a parent-teacher-student conference. If that doesn't work, get a counselor involved.

- Ask the child, "What specifically is bothering you about what the teacher does?"

- Have the teacher define his or her view of the problem, and then decide what to do.

- Support your child in moving into another class if you decide the teacher is abusive.

- Let your child know that you support her in her decision about handling this situation.

- Look at the history of both teacher and child. Is this a teacher many children have trouble with? If so, get your child moved to another teacher, and start action to protect other children. Or does your child have trouble with lots of teachers? If so, get counseling for her.

- Say, "I love you, and I will help you in whatever way you need in order to work this out."

- Talk to the school counselor to see if you can get additional information or help there.

- Figure out with your daughter what can be done; then help her do it.

- See the teacher, without your child, and take your spouse.

Thanks to Sara Monser,
Suggestion Circle from Lafayette, California

97. My fifteen-year-old is a truant from high school and lies about it.

- Find out why he is missing school, give him family consequences, and confront the lies with facts.

- Involve a third party, such as a school or family counselor, in a discussion of the problem.

- Ask him what he plans to do about the future and this problem.

- Tell him he is important and that it's important for you to understand why he's truant and why he lies.

- Tell him what the consequences will be if he's truant or lies again. Follow through.

- Tell him you will ask the school to call you if he is late or absent.

- Expect honesty, and figure out if you have been punishing honesty.

- Share your concern with your other children, and see if they know what's going on with the child.

- Ask him about his goals for his life and how education fits into his achieving those goals.

- Look for ways you can get involved at school.

- Ask him what happens to people who are truant and who lie when they are ages twenty and twenty-five.

- Consider the possibility of drug abuse by him or someone in the family system.

(See also questions 122, 123, 127, and 132.)

Thanks to Jean Clarke,
Suggestion Circle from Minnetonka, Minnesota

98. We are moving to a different town. My sixteen-year-old child is scared and acting out. What can we do?

- Give her a lot of love. Make sure she knows what's going to happen next.

- Invite a friend of hers to come and spend a week or two with you after you move.

- Provide as much certainty as possible in her life.

- Take your daughter along when you go to look for a new home and to visit the schools.

- Sit down as a family and talk about how each person feels about the move.

- Contact someone in the new area who has a child the same age as your child. Introduce them.

- She didn't make the decision to move. Help her identify all the things that she *can* make decisions about.

- Say, "Honey, I'm scared, too. Let's make a list together of sixteen ways you and I can help each other get past our fears." Read the chapter on support groups in Clarke's *Self-Esteem: A Family Affair*. (See "Resources.")

- If she is currently in a good school and social situation, consider finding a family for her to live with while she finishes the school year.

(See also "Ages and Stages," "Affirmations for Growth—Identity, Sexuality, and Separation," and *Help for Kids! Understanding Your Feelings About Moving*, by Gesme and Peterson. See "Resources.")

Thanks to Samara Kemp,
Suggestion Circle from Modesto, California

99. My two teens are out of school at 2:00. I don't get home till 6:00. When I ask what they have been doing, they say, "Nothing." I'm worried. What can I do?

- Encourage them to join school clubs, sports, hobby groups, or after-school classes. Support their choices and involvement however you can.

- Contact the local youth or recreation department for ideas of classes, sports, or projects your teens can become involved in.

- Share your concerns with your kids, and listen to their ideas and feelings.

- Reduce your work hours so you can be home when they get out of school, if you can.

- Contract with your teens to do repairs or projects around the house during after-school hours.

- Be sure some caring adult is around. These kids still need adults for stability.

- Let them know that you expect them to use that time for study, work, or recreation that is constructive.

- Can they get part-time jobs?

- If your concern includes possible sexual activity, be sure a housekeeper, relative, or tutor is in the house when teens are home.

Thanks to Sara Monser,
Suggestion Circle from Lafayette, California

Chapter 11

Drugs, Sex, and Health

100. How do I say no to my child who wants to go to a party where alcohol and drugs will be used?

- Say no and offer another option, such as inviting her friends to your house.

- Say no onto a tape recorder. Listen to the tone of your voice to see if you might be inviting your child to argue.

- Stand in front of your mirror and practice saying no in different body positions and tones of voice. Don't smile when you say it to her.

- Gather other parents and friends together to support you. Practice with each other.

- Say, "Because I trust you, saying no is hard for me. Because I care, 'no' it is."

- Figure out what makes it so difficult for you to say no.

- Look up "no" in six different languages. Use them all!

- Practice saying no in other areas of your life.

- Use your vocal cords and say, "No!"

- If your child is underage, say, "No. It is against the law for you to consume alcohol. Drugs are illegal."

(See also questions 101 and 102.)

Thanks to Sara Monser,
Suggestion Circle from Concord, California

101. What kind of rules should I set for my sixteen-year-old daughter regarding drinking and driving?

- If she does drink at a party, set a rule that she is to call home for a ride.

- Make an absolute rule about no drinking and driving.

- Listen to her feelings about drinking, and stay firm on your rule that drinking is not permitted until she is of legal age.

- Say, "If you drink, I will take away your privileges." Let her know you'll provide a ride home if for any reason she will be unsafe in a car.

- Have her call you or a sober friend for a ride if anyone is drinking and driving.

- Say, "Drinking is illegal for underage children. You may not drink alcoholic beverages."

- Each of you sign a contract stating that neither of you will drink if you must drive.

- Think about what rules you feel are appropriate for a child in your family; then state them clearly to her and enforce them.

- Read *Steering Clear: Helping Your Child Through the High-Risk Drug Years*, by Cretcher. (See "Resources.")

- "If you drink, don't drive."

- "If you drink when you have the car, you are grounded for three months."

  (See also question 100.)

Thanks to Sara Monser,
Suggestion Circle from Lafayette, California

102. I think my seventeen-year-old is drinking too much. What can I do?

- Say, "Stop! Drinking is against the law at your age. You must not drink."

- Abuse of one substance often leads to other substance abuse. Get him evaluated immediately by a substance abuse agency.

- Recount to him specific actions that have caused you to become concerned. You are the parent. Set rules and consequences.

- Think about whether there is anything you do that encourages him to drink, such as covering for him.

- Read *An Elephant in the Living Room,* by Marion Typpo and Jill Hastings. It talks about how to cut through denial. (See "Resources.")

- Get in touch with Alcoholics Anonymous, the hot line in your city, or the National Council on Alcoholism.

- Call your local alcohol treatment center for information and actual help with confronting his behavior.

- Tell him that young people develop cirrhosis of the liver, which is eventually fatal, from drinking an amount of alcohol much smaller than that which affects adults and that the disease progresses faster in teens than it does in adults.

(See also questions 100, 132, and "Where to Go for Additional Support.")

Thanks to Harold Nordeman,
Suggestion Circle from Cincinnati, Ohio

103. I just learned that my nineteen-year-old niece, who had been through alcohol treatment, has started drinking again. What can I do to help?

- Go to her, tell her what you have heard, and ask her if it is true. Ask if there is anything you can do to help.

- Call your sister-in-law and brother, and offer to be a support to them if they will tell you what they need.

- Let your brother know that you love him and that you know about his daughter's drinking again.

- Suggest a qualified assessment to find out the degree of her abuse.

- See a film on alcoholism. Learn all you can. Take action on the information.

- Attend an Al-Anon meeting tonight.

- Get information on drug abuse. Confront; don't gloss over it.

- Invite your brother and sister-in-law to go to an Al-Anon meeting with you.

- Learn about alcoholism, and see if you are contributing to the problem in any way.

- Evaluate your relationship with her. Do whatever you can to help support her sobriety.

- Tell her how you are feeling, and invite her to share her feelings.

(See also question 102 and "Where to Go for Additional Support.")

Thanks to Carole Gesme,
Suggestion Circle from Minneapolis, Minnesota

104. I think my teenagers may be using drugs. What are some clues? How can I find out about it?

- Ask them.

- Go to community programs that offer information on drugs. Your local alcohol council may have information, files, handouts, and so on.

- Observe what kind of friends they are hanging around with. This is often a telling clue.

- Look for school problems or for sudden changes in mood or behavior.

- If they are evasive and reclusive, this may be a clue that they are using drugs.

- If your kids have more problems in general than they usually have, this may be a clue.

- Red eyes, runny nose, and changes in pupil size, appetite, sleep patterns, and grooming are frequent clues.

- Do they look as if they crawled out from under a rock?

- Refusal to discuss things with you may be a clue.

- Read *Not My Kid*, by Polson and Newton, or *Getting Tough on Gateway Drugs: A Guide for the Family*, by DuPont. (See "Resources.")

(See also question 105 and "Where to Go for Additional Support.")

Thanks to Carol Gesme,
Suggestion Circle from Minneapolis, Minnesota

105. My child is smoking pot. What shall I do?

- Be prepared to enforce anything you say you will do.

- Get the support of other parents.
- Contact the local law enforcement agency to find out the law in your community.
- Act now. Tomorrow he could try the heavier stuff.
- Ask him what he gets out of it, and suggest that he find healthy highs like running or getting involved in an exciting hobby or activity. Back him all the way.
- Get an evaluation by a drug abuse agency.
- Try therapy.
- Say, "Stop." Put a time limit on it, and if he hasn't stopped by that time, he goes into treatment.
- Have him talk to a peer who is recovering from chemical dependency.
- Separate the behavior from the person. Tell him that you love him and that he has to stop smoking dope.
- Have him attend Narcotics Anonymous meetings.
- Write to the National Institute on Drug Abuse for *Parents: What Can You Do About Drug Abuse?* (See "Resources.")

(See also questions 100, 104, 132, and "Where to Go for Additional Support.")

Thanks to Julia Moen,
Suggestion Circle from Minneapolis, Minnesota

106. My son wants to have his girlfriend in his room with him "to listen to records." What should I do?

- Tell him to keep the door open.
- Tell them OK, and you will bring some snacks up to them. Then do it and continue to look in on them frequently.
- Say, "Bring your records down to the family room."

- Say, "No, it is inappropriate in our home for a young man to have a young woman in his room."

- Tell him, "Yes, it's OK, as long as you will keep it friendly and set limits on your own and her behavior."

- Figure how to set up another space in the house for them where you can respect their privacy.

- Set a limit on the amount of time they can spend alone in the bedroom.

- Explain that the bedroom has sexual implications for couples who are attracted to each other. Don't let him do it.

- Find out why the bedroom is so important to him. If you feel convinced that the reasons are valid and that he can handle the situation competently, consider allowing it.

(See also questions 111 and 132.)

Thanks to Gail Nordeman,
Suggestion Circle from Cincinnati, Ohio

107. My daughter and her boyfriend can't keep their hands off each other. She is only fourteen. What can I do?

- It sounds like she needs limits. Say, "All this touching is not appropriate for someone your age. Do you need to stop seeing this boy, or can you keep your touching within safe limits?"

- Read Ruth Bell's *Changing Bodies, Changing Lives* or *Puberty: An Illustrated Manual for Parents and Daughters*, by Angela Hynes, with her. (See "Resources.")

- Find out if she is doing what her boyfriend wants just to please him and because she's afraid of losing him.

- Accept her excitement; then help her set limits and find other things to do with her boyfriend.

- Move.
- Make sure you discuss with her the consequences of intercourse: babies, abortions, feeling loved, commitment, disappointment, and venereal disease.
- Are they having intercourse? If they are, take action to get it stopped. She is too young for this. The loss of innocence can affect them for the rest of their lives.
- Talk with her about the difference between nurturing touch and sexual touch. Increase the amount of nurturing touch you are offering her.

(See also questions 108, 132, 137, "Ages and Stages," and "Structuring for Responsibility and Independence.")

Thanks to Sara Monser,
Suggestion Circle from Lafayette, California

108. I think my teenager may be sexually active. We've never talked about sex at all. How do I initiate talks about birth control, social problems, and diseases?

- Say, "Please read *The New Teenage Body Book*, by McCoy and Wibbelsman, or *Changing Bodies, Changing Lives*, by Ruth Bell. In a few days, I'll be asking what you think of the contents." (See "Resources.")
- Together or separately watch the video "Time Out" with Magic Johnson and Arsenio Hall. Talk about it.
- Give him *The Facts of Love*, by Alex and Jane Comfort, or *Why Love Is Not Enough*, by Sol Gordon. Talk about it later. (See "Resources.")
- Listen to how he's feeling and don't criticize.
- Ask him, "What place do you think sex has in a love relationship?"

- Start now. Talk about sex, love, bonding, marriage, and commitment.
- Tell him you are concerned about AIDS.
- Ask him what sex means to him—socially, physically, emotionally—and discuss the possible consequences.
- Be comfortable with your own sexuality, so you can talk with him and he with you.

(See also questions 107, 132, 140, 142, "Ages and Stages," and "Safer Sex.")

Thanks to Sara Monser,
Suggestion Circle from Concord, California

109. I found birth control pills in my fourteen-year-old daughter's room. What should I do?

- Find out if she is using them or not and if she is having intercourse or not.
- Tell her you love her and are concerned.
- Tell her she's too young emotionally to have intercourse.
- Take action! Get help.
- Remind her that her body is hers and is not to be used to please someone else.
- Look with her at statistics on the relation of cervical cancer to early intercourse, the ineffectiveness of the pill, and the prevalence of diseases. The Pill does not prevent AIDS!
- Look to see if the limits and rules at your house are too rigid or too loose. *You* set the standards.
- Get help from a family counselor.
- Look for the possibility of too little nurturing touch at your house or the possibility of sexual molesting. Get counseling.

- Talk to her about the role of intercourse in a committed love relationship, and tell her that she is too young for this.

- Give her *What's Happening to My Body?*, by the Madarases. You read *Talking with Your Teenager*, by Bell and Zeiger. (See "Resources.")

(See also questions 108, 116, 132, "Ages and Stages," and "Affirmations for Growth—Identity, Sexuality, and Separation," and "Safer Sex.")

Thanks to Sara Monser,
Suggestion Circle from Lafayette, California

110. I found my seventeen-year-old daughter's birth control pills. What should I say?

- Say, "I found your birth control pills. Let's talk."

- Affirm her responsibility in taking precautions, then ask about her plans for a career, marriage, and motherhood.

- Look at your daughter's relationships. Discuss lovingly their possible effects on her, including disease, pregnancy, her reputation, her own image of herself, and the long-term effects of abortion.

- Tell her how you feel and what your hopes are.

- Set your limits while she is living with you.

- Let her know you love her.

- Emphasize that the choice of sharing her body in intercourse is hers and to be done *only* for her reasons and values, not in response to someone else's wishes or to peer pressure.

- Say "We need to talk about AIDS." Give her *AIDS: What Every Student Should Know*, by Rathers and Boughn. (See "Resources.")

- Assure her that even though she has had sex, she does not have to say yes again if she chooses not to.

- Have her read *The New Our Bodies, Ourselves,* by the Boston Women's Health Book Collective, and *The Facts of Love,* by Alex and Jane Comfort. (See "Resources.")

(See also questions 109, 116, 132, "Ages and Stages," and "Structuring for Responsibility and Independence.")

Thanks to Gail Nordeman,
Suggestion Circle from Cincinnati, Ohio

111. I know my nineteen-year-old son is sleeping with his girlfriend, but I'm uncomfortable with their sharing a room when they're in my home.

- Say, "No way in our house."

- Make clear to them that your values haven't changed, and they must respect your values in your house.

- Decide what you can tolerate that will be consistent with your own values; then enforce rules to support your values.

- Tell them they need to abide by your rules in your home.

- Prepare a room for each, and if they bring up the issue of sleeping together, explain that you do not support their behavior.

- Tell your son, "I love you, and I'm uncomfortable with your sleeping in the same room. I want you to find a way to honor my values."

- Say, "You are not married, and you may not sleep in the same room in my home."

- Insist that the friend sleep at someone else's house when your son is home.

- Decide if and when it will be OK, and then tell them your decision and what you expect from them in the meantime.

  (See also questions 100, 106, and 132.)

  Thanks to Sara Monser,
  Suggestion Circle from Lafayette, California

112. My daughter is pregnant. I am against abortion, but a baby now will destroy the life we've hoped she'd have. Help me think about it.

- Get good prenatal care for her, and see that all possibilities for a good adoptive home are investigated.

- Be aware that pregnancy can be very dangerous for a young person whose body is not mature enough to handle it.

- Consider whether abortion, as negative as it may be, might be less harmful than the other options available.

- Your daughter's wishes must be taken into account as well as yours.

- Look at what will happen to you, your child, your family, and the baby if the pregnancy goes to term.

- Have a conference with the father of the child and his family before any decision is made.

- Keep in mind that every child needs two parents and deserves to be wanted and to be raised in a whole family by loving parents. What is your daughter ready for?

- There is no quick fix. Give your daughter support in every possible way. State your views without blaming, and both of you get help and counsel.

- Your daughter has some hard choices to make. Help her all you can.

  (See also questions 132, 168, and "Ages and Stages.")

  Thanks to Sara Monser,
  Suggestion Circle from Lafayette, California

113. My daughter is so thin I'm afraid she's anorexic. What should I do?

- Take her to her doctor for a physical to see if her weight is within normal range for her age and height.
- Look in the phone book for an eating disorders clinic. Make an appointment for an evaluation—now!
- Share with her your concern, and figure out together what each of you can do.
- Tell her you love her.
- Monitor her eating habits. Look for diet pills, laxatives, diuretics, or other drugs. Notice whether she is exercising compulsively and if her menstrual periods have stopped. Ask your doctor for help.
- Get help from people who know about anorexia.
- Affirm her as a woman, and let her know it's OK for her to grow up.
- Ask her how she sees herself, and discuss how women are portrayed in the media.
- Decide if you may be expecting perfection from her. If so, take the pressure off. Love her as she is, warts and all.
- If she is anorexic, recognize the suicidal aspect of her behavior. Ask her to make a commitment to live. Get help.

- Read Steven Levenkron's *The Best Little Girl in the World* or other books on anorexia. (See "Resources.")

Thanks to Gail Nordeman,
Suggestion Circle from Cincinnati, Ohio

114. My daughter was raped. I don't know what to do to help her.

- Tell her that you love her, and look for expert help for her, for yourself, and for your family.

- Call your minister, family physician, and the rape crisis center for help.

- Accept the situation—no denial. Don't blame her. Let her know you love and honor her. Then call whomever you need to get counsel and help.

- Ask her how she feels about it, and accept all of her feelings. She may need to talk about it many times, and you may, too.

- Take immediate action—take her to the hospital. Call the police. Decide later if you want to prosecute.

- She may be feeling guilty. She is not to blame even if it was a date rape. Learn about victim blame, and guard carefully against it.

- Make sure she knows that this was a crime of sexual violence and that the attacker bears the entire blame.

- Release any excess anger with a counselor, not against any member of your family. Use your anger to think about and resolve the problem.

- It is important for her to separate this violent sexual act from her own sexuality. Make clear to her that this was a misuse of power.

- She needs a male family member to take her side. Read *If She Is Raped*, by McEvoy and Brookings. (See "Resources.")

Thanks to Harold Nordeman,
Suggestion Circle from Cincinnati, Ohio

115. I just found out that my daughter was sexually abused by a cousin when she was five. How can I support her now?

- Be available to listen to her and talk with her. This is serious even if she doesn't want to talk about it.

- Find a therapist who specializes in sexual abuse issues, and get your daughter and yourself into treatment! Remember that you are a secondary victim.

- Assure your daughter over and over that the experience has not made her less OK and that she was not to blame.

- Hold her in your arms and say, "I'm sorry that happened. If I had known, I would have protected you."

- Make sure that the cousin isn't still able to molest little girls. Do this however you need to, and let your daughter know you're doing it.

- Separate your own sorrow about not having been able to protect her and your anger toward your relative.

- Find a support group of other teens who have had similar experiences. They can help heal each other.

- Buy her a copy of *The New Our Bodies, Ourselves*, by the Boston Women's Health Book Collective, and read together the parts about violence against women. (See "Resources.")

- Send her to a self-defense class, such as "Powerful Choices" or "Model Mugging," so she has the power to protect herself in the future. You go, too.

Thanks to Sara Monser,
Suggestion Circle from Lafayette, California

116. How can I help my daughter and my son to know how urgent it is for people to use condoms as protection against STDs (sexually transmitted diseases) and HIV/AIDS (human immune deficiency virus/acquired immune deficiency syndrome) and also that this protection is not complete?

- Be honest about the risks. AIDS is a fatal disease. It is not just a "gay" disease.

- Be well informed. You can call 1-800-342-AIDS and ask for guidelines about how to talk about AIDS. Keep the communication line with your children open.

- Ask your teens what they know about STDs, HIV/AIDS, and protection. Reinforce their appropriate knowledge, and tell them the parts they don't know.

- Emphasize that you can't get a "little" HIV. Either you have it or you don't.

- If your teen has sex, using a condom and spermicide is *absolutely* necessary, and it is still not completely safe.

- Be sure your teen knows that heterosexual adolescents are a population that has an increasingly high rate of becoming HIV positive, so the risks are going up.

- We know there isn't safe sex. I believe there is sacred sex.

- Say to them, "The only 'safe sex' is with one uninfected partner. If you have sex otherwise, a condom and spermicide are a hell of a lot better than nothing."

(See "Safer Sex.")

Thanks to Sara Monser,
Suggestion Circle from Lafayette, California

117. How do I get my son to wear a helmet when he rides his motorcycle?

- Pay for the shiniest, flashiest helmet money can buy. Most teens will wear status symbols. In addition, low-quality helmets do not protect well and may cause spinal injuries.

- Take him to a race or rally. He will see that guys who are serious about riding mostly wear helmets.

- Buy him a set of leather boots and gloves. Helmets are not enough!

- If helmets are required by law, insist that your son obey the law.

- Insist that he take a safety course. If there's no course available, organize one through the Motorcycle Safety Foundation.

- Arrange to visit a head trauma rehabilitation hospital. Include an interview with a trauma specialist.

- Wear a helmet yourself whenever you ride your bicycle.

- Tell your son you love him and you don't want him to suffer damage. Motorists often don't see motorcycles.

- Motorcycling is a dangerous activity that can be fun. Tell him that if he learns to ride well and seriously, he will be able to enjoy riding for a long time. If he does not learn to control his cycle, he will fall, get hurt, and have to quit.

- Tell him only squids (nerds) don't wear helmets.

Thanks to Sara Monser,
Suggestion Circle from Lafayette, California

118. I'm concerned about all the contact sports my child is in because of the possibility of injuries. What can I do?

- If your son follows the rules of the games, he is more likely to be safe.

- To minimize injury, help your child find a sport that best matches your child's physical abilities.

- To understand your fear, read *Feel the Fear, and Do It Anyway*, by Susan Jeffers. (See "Resources.")

- Attend sports practice sessions, and see if he is safe.

- Young bodies become strong through exercise.

- Talk to the coach about stretching and cool-downs.

- Trust your gut about whether the coach is being appropriate or inappropriate.

- Be sure you are not sending messages that injuries are manly or macho.

- Make sure protective clothing is worn for contact sports.

- Have a consultation with your child and a sports doctor to discuss your fears and the long-term effects of possible injuries for your particular child.

Thanks to Sandra Sittko,
Suggestion Circle from Saint Louis, Missouri

Chapter 12

Parent and Teen Relationships

119. What do I do when my child won't answer my questions?

- Write your question on paper, and hand it to him. Tell him you need an answer.

- Say, "Look at me. Stop what you are doing for two minutes, and respond to my questions."

- Take him to an ear doctor. He may have a hearing problem.

- Don't ask him if he will do something if you won't accept no for an answer. Just tell him to do it.

- Go to a communication class, and examine your words, tone, and gestures.

- Stand in front of him. Hold his shoulders and tell him that you are important and deserve to have an answer; then ask again.

- Say, "No answer, no weekend privileges."

- Did the secretiveness start suddenly? Have you considered that he may be on drugs?

- Look at the way you answer questions. How do you model giving answers to people in your family?

- Examine your questions. Maybe they are too intrusive.

(See also questions 122, 123, 132, and 173.)

Thanks to Deane Gradous,
Suggestion Circle from Saint Paul, Minnesota

120. My thirteen-year-old wants to take over as parent. What can I do?

- Have a family meeting and define roles.
- Say, "I appreciate good thinking, but *I* will do the parenting."
- Say, "You don't need to take care of me."
- Say, "Thanks for the offer, but I'll keep my job as parent."
- Ask the child questions about what caretaker jobs each of you will be responsible for.
- Talk about responsible roles for different ages of people.
- If she wants a pet, buy her one to care for.
- Look for a variety of ways to express love. You retain the parent role.
- Examine your own behavior to see if there are ways in which you are unconsciously asking your child to take care of you.
- Let your child take over some tasks that support the whole family, such as meal planning, shopping, or keeping one room clean.
- Set aside ten minutes a day for your child to give family members "parent" suggestions and criticisms. That is all.

(See also question 170 and "Parents of Teenagers Get Another Chance—Recycling.")

Thanks to Darlene Montz,
Suggestion Circle from Yakima, Washington

121. How can I deal with a thirteen-year-old who has become very sassy and critical?

- Restate what she says in a clear, kind way. Ask her if that was what she meant to say.

- While you tell her your feelings about her sassiness, remember how important it is for thirteen-year-olds to get lots of love and Being messages. (See "Developmental Affirmations for All Ages.")

- Charge her a fee each time she is sassy.

- Ask her to think of ways she can respond differently.

- Tell her that you intend to treat her respectfully and that you expect her to treat you the same way.

- Catch her being pleasant, and compliment her.

- This may be a temporary experiment she is trying out. Ask her.

- Don't sass her back.

- When she sasses say, "Stop. Start over and say something kind." If she doesn't, do not respond in any way.

- Say, "Ouch, that hurts!"

- Have her do something for you, such as get you a cup of coffee or give you a shoulder rub, each time she is sassy!

(See also questions 132, 135, "Ages and Stages," and "Parents of Teenagers Get Another Chance—Recycling.")

Thanks to Betty Beach,
Suggestion Circle from Plymouth, Minnesota

122. How can I let my son know how I feel when I find out that he has kept secrets about things I need to know or that he has lied to me? I want him to trust me.

- Say, "I found out this went on, and I feel left out. Next time I want to find out from *you* what happened, not in a roundabout way."

- Figure out with him a code word you can use in public to tell him that you need more information and that he should tell you at the first opportunity.

- Say, "Look here, I feel [angry, sad, worried]. I don't have all the information, and I feel mistrusted. Will you tell me what happened?"

- Don't beat around the bush. Express your frustration and expect accurate information. Find out why he doesn't trust you.

- Say, "In order to be a good parent to you, I need to know certain things. When I don't get that information, I feel scared and helpless."

- Say, "Perhaps if I had known, I could have helped."

- Ask, "Have I been worthy of your trust in the past?" If he says no, ask, "How can I earn that trust again?"

- Say, "It's OK for you to keep secrets to yourself for your own privacy. If you want to talk to me about them, I'll be available. It's not OK to lie."

- Make the consequences fit the lie.

  (See also questions 119, 132, and 173.)

Thanks to Ellen Peterson,
Suggestion Circle from Lafayette, California

123. What can I do to build a better relationship with a manipulative teen?

- When she is not manipulative, respond positively.

- Get a clear picture of how you have been a part of the problem, and change your part of it.

- Tell her directly that you are working to build a better relationship with her.

- She learned how to manipulate. Now she can learn how to get what she wants in a straightforward way. Be careful not to respond positively or to laugh or to brag about her tricks.

- Find a therapist for you both, together or separately, in order to work on the relationship.

- Tell her that her manipulation is not OK and that you expect her to change.

- Clear up any tendency *you* have to manipulate.

- Take a parenting class to learn some new options.

- When you realize you have been manipulated, complain! Don't hide it. Let her know how her behavior affects others.

- Rollo May, in *Power and Innocence*, says that manipulative power is power over another person that may have originally been invited by the other person's own desperation or anxiety. (See "Resources.")

(See also questions 119, 127, 132, 174, and "Structuring for Responsibility and Independence.")

Thanks to Judi Salts,
Suggestion Circle from Yakima, Washington

124. What do I do when my teen says "Don't act mushy in front of my friends" and doesn't want me to touch him?

- Ask what "mushy" means and how he wants you to act in front of people.

- Do any public touching only when clowning around and having fun.

- Watch for opportunities when you're alone to offer a back rub. Pat him on the back for a "good job" and such.

- Practice appropriate touching in all relationships—with family and with friends. Show him in this way that touching is OK.

- Respect his request in public, and ask before hugging or touching him in private.

- Talk about the difference between nurturing touches and sexual touches.

- Celebrate that he is in this stage of development. My boys went through it, and it didn't last long.

- Joke about it when his friends aren't around. Call after the kid, "Darn! You got away without a hug again!"

- Say, "Even though I would like to hug you, your touching needs are important, too!"

- Don't touch him. Say, "I respect your space. When you are ready for a hug or pat, let me know."

(See also question 172, "Ages and Stages," and "Affirmations for Growth—Identity, Sexuality, and Separation.")

Thanks to Ellen Peterson,
Suggestion Circle from Lafayette, California

125. Do you have developmental information and suggestions for responding to a fourteen-year-old daughter's accusations that her parents don't love her?

- Kids who are becoming separate from their parents often convince themselves that their parents are awful.

- Say, "I do love you. Even if you don't believe it right now, I do love you."

- If she is sad about giving up dependence and scared of being independent, she may be showing that by accusing you of not caring.

- Think of ways to give her more—or fewer—chances to be independent of you, whichever you think she needs.

- Intimacy and separation can sometimes be helped by friendly hassling in a way that invites all of the people involved to feel good about themselves. Clarke's *Self-Esteem: A Family Affair* discusses hassling. (See "Resources.")

- Make her a three-foot card in the shape of a heart, and write "I love you" on it. Give it to her.

- Discuss with her how she thinks parents who love their fourteen-year-olds should behave. Compare her beliefs with yours.

(See also questions 124, 176, "Ages and Stages," and "Affirmations for Growth—Identity, Sexuality, and Separation.")

Thanks to Jean Clarke,
Suggestion Circle from Minneapolis, Minnesota

126. What do I say when my child says "You don't trust me" about schoolwork and about his social life?

- Explain that trust is earned by being honest and responsible.

- Clarify that rules are designed for his safety and well-being and to minimize negative influences.

- Point out that the issue may not be one of trust but of not subjecting him to volatile situations that he may not yet have the maturity or experience to cope with.

- If the child has actually been untrustworthy, tell him what he must do to rebuild the broken trust.

- Be sure to provide a consistent role model of trustworthiness. Do what you say you will do.

- Say, "We trust you as long as you are trustworthy. If you break that trust, you must regain it by the way you behave."

- Tell him your job is gradually to shift more responsibility to him, and ask him if he is ready for some more.

- Point out that trusting himself to behave in a way that's consistent with his own goals is the most important kind of trust.

- If you don't trust him, say, "Correct. I don't trust you today. But I will as soon as you show me by your behavior that you deserve it."

(See also questions 119, 125, 132, and 173.)

Thanks to Sara Monser,
Suggestion Circle from Lafayette, California

127. My fifteen-year-old daughter has run away for short periods three times. She comes home on her own. What should I do?

- Look for the community resources that are available to help you with the problem.

- Spend more special time with her.

- Say, "Stay here and work this out with us. People learn how to get along in their families. We can help, or we will get help."

- Tell her that you love her and that her behavior is not acceptable.

- Find a counselor for her, alone or in a group.

- Get therapy for the family as a whole.

- Say, "This must stop immediately." Then take clear, positive action. Get teachers and school counselors to support your efforts, whatever you decide to do.

- Say, "You are still my responsibility; if you run away again, I will call the police."

- When she needs some space, arrange for her to stay with another family for a few days.

- In a family meeting, have each member share feelings about running away.

- Figure out with her what she's running away from or to. Brainstorm with her about possible solutions.

- Say, "I feel like running away at times, too, but I don't. We'll get help."

(See also "Where to Go for Additional Support.")

Thanks to Sara Monser,
Suggestion Circle from Concord, California

128. My kids won't participate in family activities. How should I handle this?

- Allow choices based on development. (Must the fourteen-year-old do it because the nine-year-old must?)

- Insist on participation for significant events, and give the kids a choice on other occasions.

- Talk with your children about how to maintain involvement with the family while they continue to grow and prepare to go out into the world.

- If your teens don't want to eat meals with you, together choose two times during the week when the whole family will eat together.

- Include kids in the planning of family events and outings. Sometimes do what they want to do.

- Tell them, "It's OK if you don't participate sometimes."

- Spend some time with each child as an individual and as part of the family.

- Begin to develop new interests of your own.

- Watch the interaction during family activity. If kids are being treated like second-class citizens, change that.

- As children mature, *invite* their participation because you enjoy their company and contribution rather than *demand* it as a duty.

  (See also questions 132, 137, 141, and "Ages and Stages.")

  Thanks to Maggie Lawrence,
  Suggestion Circle from Seattle, Washington

129. My daughter's grades are OK, but she works six hours every day in addition to school, so we never see her. What can I do?

- Talk to her about why she works six hours a day.

- Offer some financial help if you can.

- Tell her you miss seeing her, and arrange some time together each week.

- Arrange your schedule so you can be there when she is home.

- Think of creative ways to let her know you love her and miss her, such as making her favorite foods, leaving little notes, sewing something for her, or doing whatever is special to her.

- Plan together to go on an outing.

- Look at what you want or need from your daughter and what other sources you have for getting that need met.

- Ask your daughter, "What do you need from me at this time in your growing up?" Figure out what you will do.

- Offer her a back rub before she goes to bed. Allow time afterward for conversation with her if you are both still awake.

(See also "Ages and Stages.")

Thanks to Judy Popp,
Suggestion Circle from Yakima, Washington

130. What do I do or say to my angry thirteen-year-old adopted son, who wants to meet his natural mother?

- I am adopted. I found my birth family when I was twenty-five. I think a thirteen-year-old needs to be reassured that you won't send him back. I worried about it from ages thirteen to sixteen. Don't begin the search until early adulthood. Say, "I am your parent, and I will love you no matter what."

- Help him express his thoughts by listening carefully, without judging. Acknowledge his feelings.

- If he hasn't heard the story of his adoption and wants to know, tell him.

- If you haven't already, give him information about her but not her name.

- Suggest that he write down all the things he wants to tell or ask her. Ask him to save the paper and add to it whenever he wants to.

- Say, "I know the name of the worker who placed you. We will ask for advice. I will support your search."

- Ask him if he wants to write a letter about himself to place in the adoption file. In most states she must wait until he grows up to contact him.

- Be sure you have done your own grieving about your infertility if that was an issue.

- Read Vera Fahlberg's *Attachment and Separation* for information on bonding and testing. Read Betty Jean Lifton's *Lost and Found* on how it feels to be adopted. (See "Resources.")

(See also question 157.)

Thanks to Shirley Bullock,
Suggestion Circle from Spring Lake Park, Minnesota

131. My fifteen-year-old daughter will not speak or look directly at her stepfather, who has been here a year, unless the situation absolutely requires it. How can I work with my daughter so she will at least be respectful?

- Tell her how you feel about her behavior and specifically what you want her to do.

- Maybe she really doesn't respect him. Ask her if he has done something she finds offensive.

- Get family counseling.

- Give her definite guidelines about how to act.

- Ask her to be as respectful to your husband as she is to other people.

- Ask her stepfather to think of a way to bridge the gap between them. Does *he* respect *her*?

- Listen to how she feels about your husband; then decide together what changes you, she, and he can make.

- Tell them both that you want and expect a change.

- Stay out of the middle of their relationship, unless either one asks for help.

- Read *Stepkids: A Survival Guide for Teenagers in Stepfamilies . . . and for Stepparents Doubtful of Their Own Survival,* by Getzoff and McClenahan. (See "Resources.")

Thanks to Jeannette Hickman-Kingsley,
Suggestion Circle from Minnetonka, Minnesota

Chapter 13

Who Is in Charge of the Rules?

132. What is meant by natural and logical consequences?

- *Natural* consequences automatically follow a behavior. *Logical* consequences are related to the behavior and make sense to a person who is thinking clearly.

- Failing a course because she doesn't study is a *natural* consequence. Having to stay home on weeknights to study is a *logical* consequence of the failure.

- Losing a friend because she's rude is *natural*. Writing a letter of apology to that friend is *logical*.

- In making contracts with our kids, we spell out the *logical* consequences we will impose if the contract is not kept.

- Missing lunch at school because she forgot to take the lunch you packed is *logical*. Being hungry because she missed lunch is *natural*.

- Feeling tired is the *natural* result of walking a long distance to school. Having to walk is the *logical* result of missing the school bus.

- Taking away television privileges for fighting at school is not logical. Having a problem-solving session with the child and school and insisting that the school enforce rules about fighting are *logical* consequences.

(See "Structuring for Responsibility and Independence" and "Structuring for Success.")

Thanks to Mary Paananen,
Suggestion Circle from Seattle, Washington

133. My thirteen-year-old wants to watch television all day. I want him to watch a few quality shows. What shall I do?

- Decide with him what is a reasonable amount of television time.

- Set your limits, then discuss with your son his choices within the limits.

- Look at the TV schedule together. Negotiate limited time for TV; then discuss why he likes at least one program.

- Put an electric timer on the TV cord. Have your son set it for the one or two hours he wishes to watch.

- Talk to your son about why you want limits and how you feel about different programs.

- Have your son select priority programs, and help him identify things to do instead of watching TV.

- Turn the TV to the wall for two weeks to break the daily habit. Then negotiate times and programs.

- Watch television with him. Help him develop critical viewing by discussing each show with him as soon as it is over.

- Don't let him have a TV in his room.

(See also question 132.)

Thanks to Sandra Petty,
Suggestion Circle from Marshall, Michigan

134. My fifteen-year-old is on the phone all the time, usually in her room with the door closed and the stereo on. What should I do?

- Allow your teen to have privacy on the phone.

- Get a second phone, or get "interrupt" service so calls can come in.

- Give her an egg timer to watch. Four "three-minute eggs" per call!

- Set limits on the time of day when each person can use the phone.

- Encourage more personal meetings without the phone by recommending sports, other activities, or visits from friends.

- Let her pay for all or part of a phone of her own.

- Figure out together what the rules should be.

- Make a deal: for every half hour of private phone use, she is to give fifteen minutes of family participation in games, conversations, or sharing chores.

- Give a choice: the stereo or the phone, not both.

  (See also question 132 and "Ages and Stages.")

Thanks to Sara Monser,
Suggestion Circle from Pleasant Hill, California

135. My teens use language that is highly offensive. How can I stop this?

- Tell them your ears hurt, and the prescribed treatment is to rest them from offensive language.

- Say, "Don't talk like that. I find your language highly offensive."

- Ask them to define the words they use.

- As you walk out of the room, tell them you will not subject yourself to that language.

- Say, "Powerful people don't need to use offensive or abrasive language. You can be powerful and think before you talk."

- Put your hands over your ears. Say, "Stop."

- Ask them to look for ways in which the same feelings can be expressed without using offensive language.

- Fine them twenty-five cents a word. Then donate the money to the charity of their choice.

- Refuse to respond to any request that includes offensive language.

- Watch your own language.

- Tape the language. Ask if they are willing to listen to the tape and hear how they sound or if they prefer to stop talking that way in your presence.

(See also questions 121 and 132.)

Thanks to Gail Davenport,
Suggestion Circle from Alderwood Manor, Washington

136. My teen's room is a constant mess, and he refuses to clean it when I ask him.

- Give him a choice: clean the room and have his weekend free, or stay home on the weekend until it is clean.

- Provide positive incentives for his keeping it clean.

- Together, figure out a written chart of jobs that includes a day for cleaning his room. Let him collect points for taking care of his jobs until he has earned a reward of something that he wants.

- Hire someone to clean his room, and require that he pay for it from his allowance or money he earns from outside jobs.

- Show him how to clean a room quickly and efficiently so it's not such a big job.

- Trade jobs with him. You'll clean his room if he'll do one of your jobs.

- Look at his messy room as his problem, not yours.

- Think about what your concern is. Could it be what others might think, or is it concern about your child's lack of structure? If the concern is structure, contract with him to improve that.

- Give him responsibility for maintaining his own things and his own space.

- Close the door.

(See also questions 92, 132, and "Structuring for Responsibility and Independence.")

Thanks to Harold Nordeman,
Suggestion Circle from Cincinnati, Ohio

137. When my teen challenges me with "I don't have to do what you say; it's my life, I can do what I want," I'm unsure how much freedom I should allow and how much I should protect her.

- Say, "It *is* your life, *and* I expect you to live by certain values. Where specifically do you want more freedom?"

- Tell her it's OK to become separate, but she still can't do everything she wants.

- Discuss what might happen if each of us did only what we wanted.

- Check the rules to be sure they are appropriate for her age.

- Listen to find out if she wants more freedom or more clearness about what's important to you.

- Ask, "What is it you want to do? How will you handle the responsibility for that?"

- Stay open to your child's hopes, dreams, and rebellions, and set limits if her monologue doesn't allow for dialogue.

- Remember that teens often need to test for limits. Decide on your important limits, and be firm about them.

- Sometime each day let her know that you love her.

- Say, "None of us can do only what we want. Follow the rules."

- Say, "It is important to learn to be cooperative as well as independent."

(See also questions 132, 140, and "Ages and Stages.")

Thanks to Sara Monser,
Suggestion Circle from Lafayette, California

138. My husband's daughter bounces back and forth between our house and her mother's because she won't abide by the rules in either household. What should I do?

- Get all adults involved to agree on a set of rules to be enforced consistently in both households. Then carry them out.

- Develop with her a written contract listing the benefits of living with you. Agree on the rules of the household and the consequences of breaking the rules.

- Insist that she think about how her actions are affecting the lives of others around her.

- Use the Yorks' *Toughlove* guidelines if the child needs a drastic change to get her attention. (See "Resources.")

- Be sure you and your husband are clear and united in your approach to rules.

- Ask her to participate in setting household rules that are acceptable to you and to help in establishing consequences.

- Keep rules as few and basic as possible in order to allow consistent enforcement.

(See also questions 132, 137, "Structuring for Responsibility and Independence," and "How to Make and Enforce Rules.")

Thanks to Sara Monser,
Suggestion Circle from Lafayette, California

139. Our sixteen-year-old daughter smokes cigarettes. We disapprove. How do we set house rules, and what rules can we set?

- Set a rule of no smoking in the house. Set consequences if she is caught smoking or if cigarettes are found in the house.

- Tell her if she must smoke, she must smoke outside.

- Say, "I am opposed to smoking. If you are going to smoke, it must be outside of our house."

- Say, "Your body is important. Smoking is hard on it. I will not be a part of your smoking. You may not smoke in the house."

- Say, "Nonsmokers inhale lots of smoke when others smoke. You may not damage my body by smoking in the house."
- Say, "In this state, it is illegal to buy cigarettes at your age. No smoking until you are eighteen!"
- Post the rules, and enforce them with penalties for breaking them such as grounding, fines, or removal of driving privileges.
- Stay alert. Young smokers sometimes move next to drinking, then drugs.
- Model no smoking: if you smoke, stop.

  (See also questions 100, 132, and 142.)

  Thanks to Julia Moen,
  Suggestion Circle from Minneapolis, Minnesota

Chapter 14

Peers, Friends, and Loves

140. How do I respond when my daughter says, "Everyone is doing it"?

- Say, *"Everyone???"*
- Say, "You can set a precedent."
- Find out what specifically she wants to do, and figure out if she can do it safely.
- Ask her to think of five other reasons to do it besides "everyone is doing it," and then you'll discuss it with her.
- Ask her to look at all the beautiful ways in which she is not "everyone" and how she can decide for herself what is right for her.
- Tell a story of someone her age who didn't do what "everyone" did and was better for it.
- Give her the affirmations for Structure. (See "Affirmations for Growth—Structure.")
- Say, "I'm not sure about that. If you insist, I'll call six mothers of your friends, and ask if their girls can do this."
- Check with her school counselor to find out how many are really doing it.
- Say, "I bet it seems that way. How many people do you count in 'everyone'?"

- Kids this age need to belong. Help her to belong and to be unique at the same time.

(See also questions 100, 132, 141, 142, "Ages and Stages," and "Structuring for Responsibility and Independence.")

Thanks to Sara Monser,
Suggestion Circle from Lafayette, California

141. I don't like my son's friends. He's always out with them, and I feel I don't have much influence on him anymore.

- Keep track of the hours he is away and the hours he's at home to see if he is gone excessively or if it just feels like it to you.

- Support positive activities that your son is interested in. Support these interests with your presence as well as your money, transportation, and time.

- Tell your child *why* you don't like his friends.

- Talk to his school counselor and teachers about the situation.

- Read *How to Talk So Kids Will Listen and Listen So Kids Will Talk,* by Faber and Mazlish. (See "Resources.")

- Ask your son to think about what his friends will probably be doing ten years from now, and ask if that's what he wants for himself.

- Support what your son does well so he sees himself as worthwhile. Friends reflect a child's needs.

- Keep the refrigerator well stocked, and you may see more of your son and his friends, too! Look for their positive points, and comment on them.

- Decide if this is your problem or your son's, since it is time for him to start separating from you. Are you ready to let him go?

(See also questions 140, 142, and "Ages and Stages.")

Thanks to Harold Nordeman,
Suggestion Circle from Cincinnati, Ohio

142. My fifteen-year-old child's friends all smoke, and she feels immature when she refuses to smoke. How can I help her?

- Praise her for being mature enough to make her own choices.

- Stress the importance of being an individual in a world that is constantly attempting to get you to conform.

- Give her special privileges for her decision not to smoke.

- Use affirmations with her: "You can find a way of doing things that works for you." (See "Affirmations for Growth—Structure.")

- Show her the research that supports the wisdom of her choice.

- Suggest that she may be the person the others will imitate in time.

- Talk with her about what "mature" means; use her choice as an illustration of mature behavior.

- Hug her often when she hasn't been with her smoking friends, and tell her how nice she smells.

- Wonder with her why people choose to smoke.

- Tell her to come and talk to you about it whenever she needs to.

- Compliment her on her mature ability to have friends who differ from her.

- Be clear about your no-smoking rule.

(See also question 139, "Ages and Stages," and "Structuring for Responsibility and Independence.")

Thanks to Judy Popp,
Suggestion Circle from Yakima, Washington

143. How do I get my teens to come home for snacks and further partying after dances and shows rather than going to a "joint" or parking?

- Tell them they are welcome to bring their friends home.

- Don't "hang out" with them when they come home. Greet them, and then disappear without leaving the house.

- Have a refrigerator full of food and soft drinks.

- Offer videotapes, records, and games.

- Talk with their friends. Get to know them. Be friendly.

- Provide an affirming environment for teens by being friendly and giving them space in the house separate from the rest of the family.

- Cultivate an attitude that is inviting and that makes clear that the kids are not a bother.

- Have the kids come over ahead of time to clean up and decorate for the party after the dance.

- Invite the group back the next day to return the house to its original condition.

- Figure out with your kids ways to make home after dates better than "joints" or parking.

- Look for ways to have fun with your teens much of the time so they prefer to come home where they feel good.

Thanks to Deane Gradous,
Suggestion Circle from Saint Paul, Minnesota

144. My sixteen-year-old daughter has made arrangements to travel with her boyfriend to visit a prospective college that is seven hours away. I don't think it's a good idea for the two of them to drive that far and spend the night. What should I tell my daughter?

- Say, "We don't agree with the two of you going together. We will take you, and your boyfriend is welcome to come along."

- Suggest that you and your daughter go together.

- Reschedule the trip so that a parent or an older brother or sister can see the school and help with the driving.

- It's all right for you as her parent to say no.

- Discuss your concerns and find out how *she* views the trip. Let her know that you expect her to use good judgment.

- It is time to talk about next year's college, away-from-home rules, and how she plans to cope with pressures to have sex.

- Plan a trip with her so you all—parents, too—can see several colleges that she's interested in, all on one trip.

(See also questions 108, 111, 132, and "Structuring for Responsibility and Independence.")

Thanks to Sandy Keiser,
Suggestion Circle from Cincinnati, Ohio

145. Our teenager wants to get married so he and his girlfriend can be together while they are in college. I think they are too young. What should I do?

- Since you think they are too young, say so and tell them why.

- Ask questions like "What will you do if you have a baby? How will you support yourselves? What about continuing your educations?"

- Figure out a way to help him without his entering into marriage.

- All involved have a session with a family counselor.

- If they are sexually active, see that they have accurate birth control information and access to the products through clinics or doctors.

- Accept their sexual desires and growing love, and talk with them about the commitment. Are they ready for that?

- Listen to their hopes and dreams, and help them figure out the best way to achieve them.

- Explain that if they love each other, their love will grow whether they are married or not.

- Let him know if you are willing to continue giving the same, more, or less financial support if he marries.

- Ask them to think what each of them will be like at thirty if they marry now or if they marry later.

(See also questions 111, 132, 144, and "Ages and Stages.")

Thanks to Gail Nordeman,
Suggestion Circle from Healdsburg, California

146. My eighteen-year-old wants to live with her boyfriend at college. How do I handle this?

- Thank her for talking with you about it. Tell her how you prefer that she behave and that you'll love her whatever she does.

- Consider that she may be asking you to say no. Otherwise she might not have asked.

- Say no and help her figure out how she can tell her friend no.

- If you have strong feelings against it, say no.

- Ask, "If you live together, which of you will be responsible for birth control?"

- Ask, "Why do you want to do this?" Discuss the options; then decide how to handle it.

- Remind her that she'll be setting an example for her younger siblings. She may want to know what has happened with other couples in order to learn from their example, just as her sibs will learn from hers.

- Point out that this is an adult decision and, as such, means she must assume the other responsibilities of adulthood.

- Have her boyfriend in on the discussion about the pros and cons of the arrangement, and share how you think and feel about it.

(See also questions 111, 112, 132, 145, and "Structuring for Responsibility and Independence.")

Thanks to Sara Monser,
Suggestion Circle from Lafayette, California

Chapter 15

Curfews, Cars, and Chores

147. My fourteen-year-old daughter wants to stay out later than midnight. What shall I do?

- Say, "Yes, you may stay out past midnight. Your new curfew is 12:10. Not a *moment* past!"

- Each June when school is out, increase the time she can stay out.

- If you live in an area that has a curfew law, obey it.

- Have her call you when she gets to the party and finds out what the party is like. Then decide on a time you both think is appropriate.

- Evaluate each event, and set the curfew accordingly.

- Tell her she can't.

- Invite her to bring friends home if she wants to continue to party past midnight.

- Discuss with her a set of rules about curfews, based on events and peer groups, that is agreeable for both of you.

- Base curfew decisions on your child's overall demonstration of good judgment.

- Allow her to stay later at a friend's house if there are chaperons.

  (See also question 93.)

  Thanks to Harold Nordeman,
  Suggestion Circle from Cincinnati, Ohio

148. I worry when my sixteen-year-old son is late. He apologizes and thinks that should end it. How can I let him know what I expect of him?

- Tell him, "I expect you to be here when you say you will be."

- Tell him you're concerned about him because you love him, and when he doesn't let you know when he's going to be late, you're afraid something has happened to him.

- Tell him, "I don't like being left without contact. If you will be more than half an hour late, call me and let me know where you are and what is happening."

- Say, "I expect you to provide two hours of fun with me to make up for the worrying I did."

- Look at your expectations to see if they are realistic. Then clarify curfews so there is no misunderstanding of expectations.

- The next time *you* are late, ask him how he feels. Think about whether this is a pattern for you and what effect it has on him.

- After you let him know what you expect, set consequences. Carry them through every time.

- Notice when he is on time or early. Praise him for the positive behavior.

(See also questions 92, 132, and 137.)

Thanks to Sandra Sittko,
Suggestion Circle from Saint Louis, Missouri

149. My daughter has no license, and she drove a car. What shall I do?

- Say, "Stop! It's illegal to drive without a license. Call me when you need transportation."

- Say, "Wait until you have your license."
- Ground her for two weeks.
- Say, "I care about you. Don't do that again."
- Say, "You could end up in the slammer."
- Say, "You have done so many creditable things. This doesn't seem like you. What's going on?"
- Sign her up for driving lessons, and tell her she can drive when she gets a license.
- See that she gets a learner's permit. Then spend quality time with her refining her driving skills.
- Say, "Think of what happens to people who disobey the law."
- Spend a day with her observing traffic court.

(See also questions 132, 137, 151, and "Structuring for Responsibility and Independence.")

Thanks to Jean Clarke,
Suggestion Circle from Bloomington, Minnesota

150. The first day my son drove the family car, he was responsible for a minor accident that cost $2,000 for repairs. How do we make this into a positive lesson?

- Have him pay the deductible or at least a portion of it so he experiences the consequences of his behavior.
- If the repairs cost $2,000, this accident doesn't sound minor. Think this through again for yourself. You might be encouraging him to disregard the seriousness of this situation.
- Have him do the footwork of getting the estimates and insurance work completed. Be available to help him if he asks.

- Until the car is repaired, limit his use of other means of family transportation.

- Have him create options for family members who need transportation, such as getting information about taxis, bus schedules, and so on.

- Look at other areas of your child's life. If he is irresponsible in other areas, get help.

- Ask him, "How could you have avoided the accident?" Make contracts about his future driving.

- Ask him how he feels. Accept his feelings, and urge him to turn the energy from his feelings into responsible action.

- Tell him you love him and that he is to drive safely.

Thanks to Sara Monser,
Suggestion Circle from Lafayette, California

151. How can I get teenagers to do kitchen duty?

- Tell them, "When you use dishes, put them in the washer."

- Suggest that they work as a team, helping each other out on days when doing the dishes is inconvenient.

- If dishwashing rules are clear, leave the dishes until they are done.

- Use the rule that they clean up their own dishes individually plus two cooking pots per person.

- If the assigned dishwasher does the dishes, then anyone finishing after that should do her own.

- See that the dishes are done before the assigned dishwasher can leave the kitchen.

- Ask kids to make out a schedule of kitchen jobs that is fairly balanced. Then encourage them to be responsible by enforcing consequences.

- Make a rule that dishes must be done sometime before those responsible go to bed. Enforce it with consequences.

- Call a family meeting for establishing a rotating schedule of household chores.

(See also questions 132, 136, and "Structuring for Responsibility and Independence.")

Thanks to Marilyn Grevstad,
Suggestion Circle from Seattle, Washington

152. I tell my fifteen-year-old son to do something at home, and he doesn't do it. How can I get him to be more responsible?

- Tell him he is important to the family and you expect his help.

- Say clearly that a job is a job even if it is at home.

- Ask him, "What do you need to handle your responsibilities at home?"

- Ask him to look at why it is a problem, and tell him what you expect from him.

- List jobs he can do. State how many you expect him to do, and tell him if he doesn't do these jobs, he can expect consequences. Then outline them.

- Decide what his reward is for completing his jobs on time.

- Allow him to experience consequences of his behavior that will inconvenience him, not you, such as no TV, no music, no access to the refrigerator, extra errands.

- If a job is supposed to be done at a certain time, be sure to enforce consequences for not meeting the deadline.

- Recognize when he is acting responsibly at home, and compliment him.

(See also questions 119, 132, 136, and "Structuring for Responsibility and Independence.")

Thanks to Suzanne Morgan,
Suggestion Circle from Albert Lea, Minnesota

Chapter 16

Identity and Self-Esteem

153. My son is short and stout, and his classmates call him names and he feels different. How can I help?

- Take him to the doctor to find out if he's in the normal range. If he is, work on self-esteem. If not, help him find a diet.

- Say, "You can learn a lot about problem solving from this situation. I'll support you."

- Point out role models from history of people who were different and succeeded.

- Teach him ways to ignore name-calling or to turn it into humor. Rehearse with him some clever (not hurtful) responses that he can use when attacked. Get Clarke's *Ouch, That Hurts!* (See "Resources.")

- Help him learn good eating habits, but let him be in charge of any weight loss.

- Point out the child's strengths and abilities, and help him focus on accepting himself rather than seeing himself as odd.

- Let him know that you love him the way he is. Have him identify ways in which other teenagers are different, too.

- If he is overweight, offer to take him to a weight-loss group, and provide wholesome food.

- Give him lots of Being messages. (See "Developmental Affirmations for All Ages.")

(See also questions 154, 155, 156, 157, and "Ages and Stages.")

Thanks to Sara Monser,
Suggestion Circle from Lafayette, California

154. My daughter is sure there is something wrong with her since she is still flat-chested at sixteen.

- Read a book together that shows pictures of different sizes and shapes. Talk about what's normal and OK. *Changing Bodies, Changing Lives,* by Ruth Bell, is a good one. (See "Resources.")

- Ask her to notice all the different breast sizes when she is in the school locker room—not just the larger ones.

- Listen carefully to her worry. Your respect for her is important.

- Assure her that her body's way of maturing has its own time schedule and that her body may have breast development way down on the agenda.

- Look with her at your family's bodies. Maybe this is genetic.

- Once she is assured of her normalcy, offer to buy her a slightly padded bra if she is self-conscious.

- If she is not yet menstruating at sixteen, she should be evaluated by her physician.

- Point out some beautiful, outstanding women in our culture who happen also to be small-breasted.

- Read *The Family Book About Sexuality*, by Calderone and Johnson, and then give it to your daughter to read. (See "Resources.")

  (See also questions 153, 155, 156, and 157.)

  Thanks to Deane Gradous,
  Suggestion Circle from Minneapolis, Minnesota

155. My teenager gets teased because he has zits. How can I help him handle the teasing?

- Tell him to say, "Hey, it's my meanness coming out. Be careful."

- Watch together the video of the movie *Mask*, which is about the elephant-man disease. The teenager in the movie handled being teased in several effective ways.

- Tell him to say, "Thank you," and change the subject.

- Tell him to smile and say, "Yes, it's a sign of raging hormones."

- Tell him how you felt when you had zits and how you handled it.

- Tell him to say, "Yeah, they are a problem. What did you use that worked?"

- Read *Ouch, That Hurts! A Handbook for People Who Hate Criticism*, by Jean Illsley Clarke. (See "Resources.")

- Tell him kids tease to cover their own insecurity and that he doesn't have to take it seriously or respond.

  Thanks to Mary Ann Lisk,
  Suggestion Circle from Minnetonka, Minnesota

156. My junior-high teen is upset by the frequent use of the words *homo*, *queer*, *les*, and *gay* as name-calling. How can I help?

- Tell her that a personal attack like this is one way kids attempt to deal with their own questions about their sexuality.

- Let her know you care for her as she is and as she is becoming.

- You might tell her about your thoughts and feelings about sexuality when you were her age.

- Talk about homosexuality factually with her, and offer to find a book to tell her more.

- Create opportunities when you are available for her to talk with you.

- Ask her if she wants the help of a counselor.

- Ask her if she knows what a lesbian is and if her friends know or if they are just doing some name-calling.

- Tell her name-calling is serious because it attacks a whole group of people and that it is not OK behavior.

- Tell her it is important for kids her age to have close same-sex friends, that they need to have those friendship bonds, and that it's your job as a parent to support her in those friendships.

(See "Ages and Stages" and "Affirmations for Growth— Identity, Sexuality, and Separation.")

Thanks to Ellen Peterson,
Suggestion Circle from Walnut Creek, California

157. Our teenage child feels so different from the rest of the family that he suspects he's adopted. I don't know how to reassure him.

- Tell him it's OK to be different and that he *is* a part of the family.

- Be sure you love him for who he is and tell him so.

- If he is adopted, tell him so.

- Reassure him that you love him, and ask him to talk with you if he needs help or feels lonely or left out.

- Tell him that as teenagers grow and separate, they sometimes feel this way and that, yes, he is your child.

- Show him his birth certificate or adoption papers. Tell him stories about his birth and infancy.

- Say, "What would help you feel better about being in our family?"

- Help him see his differences as special and wonderful, to be treasured by him just as you treasure his uniqueness.

- Perhaps he marches to a different drummer. Point out ways in which diversity enriches the family.

- If the family is sending the message, "You are OK only if you are stamped in the family mold," change that.

(See also question 130 and "Affirmations for Growth— Identity, Sexuality, and Separation.")

Thanks to Christine Ternand,
Suggestion Circle from Saint Paul, Minnesota

158. I would like suggested responses for my daughter, who wants me to feel sorry for her.

- Have her describe situations in which she used her power to effect a positive outcome. Ask her to think how she can use those qualities in this situation.

- Say, "I can't make your decisions for you, but I'm glad to be a sounding board."

- Contract for five minutes to play "oh, poor me" or "ain't it awful" games for fun to help her get it out of her system so that she can problem solve.

- Help her break the problem down into pieces and set priorities.

- Give her lots of hugs and Being messages. (See "Developmental Affirmations for All Ages.")

- Say, "I won't feel sorry for you. I *will* love you and think with you. If you want specific help from me, please ask."

- Say, "You are a powerful person. You can decide how you will resolve that situation."

- Say, "You have a lot to think about. I trust you to think clearly. Let me know how I can help you."

- Together list ten possible solutions to the situation. Include funny and ridiculous ideas as well as serious and thoughtful ones.

- Encourage her to separate facts from opinions and judgments. Ask her what you can do that would invite her to feel better about herself.

Thanks to Sue Hansen,
Suggestion Circle from Bellevue, Washington

Chapter 17

Values and Idealism

159. My junior-high child came home with seventy-dollar jeans he had got on sale for fifty dollars, and I had a fit. He couldn't understand why. He will outgrow them in a month. Help!

- Compliment him for finding a bargain. Then discuss the total amount to be spent on his clothes this year.
- Give him a clothing allowance on a weekly basis so he will have to save it up to get expensive jeans.
- Let him dress the way the other kids do if he can pay for the clothes.
- Think of this as an opportunity for you to teach him values.
- Ask him to keep track of how fast he is growing and to figure out how often he will need new clothes while he grows this fast.
- Go shopping with him, and teach him how to buy within a budget.
- Think if you have spent fifty dollars on clothes for him for a special occasion. Ask yourself if this is different.
- If you have him on a clothing allowance, this is his problem and his learning experience.

- If your family can't afford this type of expenditure, tell him so, and show him where the money is needed.

(See also question 132.)

160. Our daughter's friends are getting expensive gifts for graduation, but we don't feel we can afford an expensive gift for her. What should I do?

- Do what your values and purse dictate.

- Explain to her, "I'll be extravagant with love for you, and do the best I can with monetary gifts."

- Tell her how proud you are of her achievement, and give her the gift you can afford without apology.

- Suggest that you can come up with x dollars for what she wants, if she can come up with the rest.

- If she wants a special gift, explore with her why the gift is so important.

- Go on a fantasy shopping spree together, and share all the things you wish you could have or buy if you had unlimited funds.

- Discuss with her your whole value system—how you feel about money and how it is used.

- If you have one, give her a family heirloom or other sentimental gift.

- Offer a special gift, like a picture album or a growing-up ritual, without spending much money.

161. How do we teach our adolescents good manners, like thank-you letters and consideration of others?

- Provide personalized notepaper and stamps. Tell them to use these to write thank-you notes.

- Show them a sample thank-you note to use as a model.

- Decide if your standards are realistic for your kids' ages and situation. Be consistent in your expectations.

- Evaluate your respect and courtesy toward them, for they will learn from you how to act toward others.

- Point out specific behaviors you don't like. Make suggestions for things to do instead.

- Compliment them for the positive manners they do have.

- Let them know how good manners can ease the path for them.

- Get a good etiquette book as a gift for them.

- Talk with them about how important the consideration you receive from friends is for you.

- Occasionally "invite" your teens to be "guests" at family dinner. On other occasions, ask them to "host" a family meal. Have fun, and later discuss manners that may need improving—perhaps some of your own.

- Model what you want; allow them to overhear you comment positively when you receive a thank-you note.

Thanks to Harold Nordeman,
Suggestion Circle from Cincinnati, Ohio

162. Our son refuses to go to church with us. We believe religion is important. What can I do?

- Tell him he must go to church while he is living at home. When he's on his own, he may choose to go or not.

- Say, "You can skip church for three months. Then we will ask you to go for a month and see how it is."

- Ask him if he'd like to go to church with his friends or if he'd rather sit in a pew separate from you.

- Ask your son to investigate churches and to find one he would choose to attend. Then support his choice.

- Discuss with him when this decision will be his to make and what you expect until that time.

- See your clergy about establishing a program for teens that would fulfill their needs.

- If he says he is upset at the differences in adult behavior in church and out of church, remind him that we go to church to find ways to be better.

- If he doesn't know much about your religion, say, "We think you will need to know about your religious background. You may believe or not, but you must attend three events a month. You choose which ones."

(See also "Ages and Stages" and "Parents of Teenagers Get Another Chance—Recycling.")

Thanks to Becky Monson,
Suggestion Circle from Minnetonka, Minnesota

163. The threat of nuclear war scares our teenagers. They feel angry and depressed and feel it is useless to work for their values. What can I do?

- Help them organize a group of friends and decide on some positive action, like a letter-writing or door-to-door awareness campaign.

- Figure out with them ways to be part of peace-promoting organizations.

- Include them in family decision making, and affirm their abilities to make a difference with their participation.

- Point out to them that the threat began in 1946. Antinuclear activity has had a significant success rate, so get involved.

- Model hope for your children. Fear is paralyzing; hope is energizing.

- Look for books that reflect hope rather than doom, and all of you read them together.

- Write your representative in Congress for more information about what the government is doing to diminish the threat of war.

- Tell your children that their activity may actually make the difference.

- As a family, become involved in peace-promoting activities.

- Get *The Peace Catalogue,* by Duane Sweeney. Read it and share it with your kids. (See "Resources.")

  (See also question 168.)

Thanks to Sara Monser,
Suggestion Circle from Lafayette, California

164. How do I help my son keep his values in the face of the messages in violent movies and in many kinds of music that promote promiscuity and devalue people?

- Model respect and nonviolence consistently.

- Watch for occasions when you can honestly affirm his good judgment and discrimination.

- Have family discussions about the messages the media send viewers. Listen a lot. Don't preach. Ask how his friends react to these messages.

- Listen to the music with him, and ask him to explain the lyrics and what they mean to him. Say what they mean to you.

- Make sure you are giving your child values he can live by. Without strong values from parents, children will absorb values elsewhere.

- Discuss incidents of violence against people in our society and what you and he would like to change.

- Become a volunteer for Mothers Against Drunk Driving (MADD) or Women Against Military Madness (WAMM), and enlist his support when you need help.

- Write letters of protest to theaters and radio or TV stations, and ask who else in the family wants to sign them.

- Go to a violent movie with him. Discuss his reactions and yours.

- Do not allow violent music to be played in your house.

Thanks to Sara Monser,
Suggestion Circle form Lafayette, California

Chapter 18

Jobs, Leaving Home, the Future

165. My teen accepted a job without getting hours and pay clearly established. What can I do?

- Say, "Tell your supervisor that you didn't understand the hours and salary and that you need to go over the details again."

- Ask if she wants your help in solving this problem.

- Ask, "What do you think will happen if you continue to work without being sure what the hours and pay are?"

- Look with her at some ways she can get the information she needs. Do not offer to get the information for her.

- Say, "Talk to friends about the pay and conditions of their jobs. Then talk to your boss."

- Compliment her for getting a job, and talk over what she plans to do next.

- Tell her a story about a similar problem from your past that includes how you solved the problem.

- Say, "I'm confident you will figure out what to do about this situation and that you'll ask for help if you need it."

- Ask an older sibling to share experiences about jobs with your daughter.

- If she is often irresponsible, don't do or say anything. Let her learn from the marketplace.

(See also questions 132, 166, and "Structuring for Responsibility and Independence.")

Thanks to Melanie Weiss,
Suggestion Circle from Bellevue, Washington

166. My nineteen-year-old goes from job to job, never staying with one for more than a month or so. I'm worried how this will affect his future. What should I do?

- Find out why he is leaving his jobs. Is it because he can't get along with employers, has unrealistic expectations of the job, or what?

- Discuss with him the pattern of going from job to job and your fear that this pattern is a serious problem.

- Reduce your financial support so he has to work in order to have the things he wants.

- Evaluate what's happening at home. How much support for working does he get?

- Clarify with him his goal for working.

- Review the pattern to see if it's a pattern in his whole life, like going from friend to friend, school to school, or plan to plan for the future. If so, get counseling for him.

- Encourage him to stay with his current job for a period of time (six months), and say that you will help him work out any problem he is having there.

- If he has never worked before, don't worry if he explores jobs for the first four or five months.

- Could the problem be connected with drug abuse?

  (See also questions 104, 132, and 165.)

Thanks to Sara Monser,
Suggestion Circle from Lafayette, California

167. My daughter is in her first year at college and has been there three months. She is saying, "I want to come home. I want to quit college. I don't know what I want." What should I do?

- Ask her if she can stick it out and do her best until the end of the semester before deciding on the next step.

- See if she is willing to study for a week, then call you to tell you how she is doing.

- Ask her how she is feeling physically. Suggest a consultation at the health center.

- Tell her you love her and wish you could hug her until she felt better just as you did when she was little, and then send brownies.

- Tell her to talk to her residence assistant, adviser, counselor, pastor, or friend, and get extra help and support through the crisis.

- Ask her what she *will* do if she doesn't stay in school.

- Help her identify her areas of discomfort—schoolwork, social situations and dates, girlfriend problems, or the homesickness. Then ask her to decide on and rate which are most important and in need of attention.

- Find out how else she needs you to help with homesickness, other than coming home.

(See also "Ages and Stages" and "Affirmations for Growth — Identity, Sexuality, and Separation.")

Thanks to Deane Gradous,
Suggestion Circle from Minneapolis, Minnesota

168. What do I say or do when my teenagers say, "I have no future; there is no future for me"?

- Say, "I believe you have a future, and I care about you."

- Listen to the ways in which they are afraid. If this is about the threat of nuclear war, figure out something you can do together to promote peace. Get *The Peace Catalogue*, by Duane Sweeney. (See "Resources.")

- Tell stories of times when you felt the same way and how you handled it.

- Ask if they mean personal competence, jobs, ecology, war, or whatever, and then brainstorm for options.

- Help them develop affirmations to say to themselves. (See "Developmental Affirmations for All Ages.")

- Say, "How can I help you?"

- Mention counseling as a possible way to deal with these feelings.

- Find out in a sensitive way if this is a suicidal cry for help. If it is, get help immediately.

- Tell them that a strong religious faith can help with this problem.

- Find out what they are feeling helpless about. Ask, "What do you mean?" Listen. Say, "I love you."

- Check for drug abuse.

  (See also question 163.)

Thanks to Jean Clarke,
Suggestion Circle from Plymouth, Minnesota

169. Our teenager wants to join the Peace Corps after high school and skip college. What should I do?

- Encourage her to go for it.

- See this as possibly the best education she can get right now. Ask her to give you her time schedule for fulfilling her goal.

- Talk to her about taking a year or two of college first so she will be more valuable in the Peace Corps job.

- Ask her to talk to a school counselor and let you know what advice she gets.

- Encourage her to get involved in community activities as a volunteer for a summer; then review the Peace Corps option.

- Go as a family to an informational seminar on the Peace Corps.

- Say, "We love you and trust you to make good decisions about your life."

- Since the Peace Corps prefers experienced people, be prepared to look at other nonacademic options with her.

- Ask her to finish college first.

- Ask her to go to college when she comes back.

- Be proud that you have raised such a caring, courageous daughter.

- Trust her.

(See also "Ages and Stages" and "Parents of Teenagers Get Another Chance—Recycling.")

Thanks to Harold Nordeman,
Suggestion Circle from Cincinnati, Ohio

Chapter 19

Parents Have Problems, Too

170. What can I do to raise my own self-esteem?

- Take a break. Sing a song. Take a bath. Take a fantasy trip. Change clothes.

- Schedule cheerleading sessions for yourself, and ask other people to cheer for you also.

- Think about how you can live by these three guidelines: love myself unequivocally; love others generously; be responsible for my part and my part only.

- Spend time with people who affirm you. Avoid those who depreciate you. (See "Affirmations for Growth.")

- Work outdoors alone or with someone. Go for a long walk, and concentrate on the beauty.

- Accept the fact that sometimes people feel low. Let it happen. Think what you can do to make those situations different next time.

- Keep notes and letters that are complimentary. Read them often.

- Learn a new skill and enjoy it.

- Write down twenty-two positive adjectives that describe you. Post them on your bathroom mirror and refrigerator door.

- Join a group that interests you, and volunteer for a job you like.

- Read Clarke's *Self-Esteem: A Family Affair.* (See "Resources.")

(See also "Parents Get Another Chance—Recycling.")

Thanks to Sue Hansen,
Suggestion Circle from Bellevue, Washington

171. I want to know how to respond to those who say to me, "Don't rock the boat. Don't grow; don't change."

- Say, "I'm a natural, growing person."
- Sing the song, "I Gotta Be Me."
- Say, "It's OK for me to learn and grow."
- Tell them you will continue to care about them as you grow and change.
- Ask them to watch what happens when you grow and change. They may decide to try it!
- Say, "I hear your concerns, but it's too painful for me to stay this way."
- Say, "You may like me even better!"
- Say nothing. Hug them.
- Say, "Do you want to see me atrophy right here in front of you?"
- Say, "Too late—I've already started," with lightness in your voice.
- Tell them that adults have developmental tasks to do and that you are an adult.

(See also "Parents of Teenagers Get Another Chance—Recycling.")

Thanks to Lois White,
Suggestion Circle from Plymouth, Minnesota

172. My teenage child considers me an embarrassment. What do I do?

- Keep a sense of humor. Don't be hurt by his separating.

- Listen carefully to his feelings. Do not be defensive. Consider what he says, and look at how you may contribute to his embarrassment.

- Be consistent in your behavior with your child. Tell him what he can expect of you in different situations.

- Acknowledge his discomfort and state, "It is appropriate for me to be here, doing this" (if it is).

- Discuss what he expects of you before situations in which he might feel embarrassed.

- Clean up your act. If your child is embarrassed because of inappropriate behavior (you are dressed in your robe in front of his friends, you drink too much alcohol, and so on), *change.*

- If you are willing to change your behavior, go along with him.

- Avoid scolding or other inappropriate behavior in front of his friends.

- Remember that many teenagers feel this way no matter what their parents do.

- *Do* insist he continue to participate in important family functions. *Do not* expect to go to the movies with him on Friday night.

(See also question 124 and "Ages and Stages.")

Thanks to Sara Monser,
Suggestion Circle from Lafayette, California

173. How can I communicate with my fourteen-year-old without losing my temper when she is going out and won't tell me where?

- Practice in front of a mirror saying calmly, "You can't go until you tell me where you are going."

- Tell her, "Your safety is important to me, and I need to know."

- When you are both calm, brainstorm with her about how to improve communication.

- Tell her to wait five minutes. Go in the bedroom and hit the pillow. Then, when you're calm, talk to her.

- Take a deep breath, speak slowly, and tell her what you want from her.

- Ask your spouse to take over for a few minutes while you breathe deeply and center yourself.

- During a time when you both are feeling good, discuss with her the responsibility that goes with living in a family, which includes letting each other know where we go.

- Ask her to call and tell you where she is when she gets there.

- Tell her why you are angry, and ask her to help.

- If underneath the anger, you are scared, tell her that.

- Be sure you tell her where *you* are going.

(See also question 119 and "Parents of Teenagers Get Another Chance—Recycling.")

Thanks to Carole Gesme,
Suggestion Circle from Wayzata, Minnesota

174. I'm afraid to say no to my teenager because he will break the furniture or hit me. What can I do?

- Tell him if he ever threatens you or strikes you again, you will call the police, and do it.

- Say, "Hitting is not allowed in this home. Do not ever threaten me with violence."

- Say a *firm* "Don't" from a this-is-the-way-it-is position.

- Tell him six ways that he can let out his anger that do not threaten you, such as yell (not at you), run, play tennis, hit the beanbag chair, and so on.

- Both of you get into counseling in a hurry.

- Find out if he is abusing drugs.

- If you or your spouse breaks furniture or hits people, do whatever you need to do to stop that.

- Affirm yourself as a parent and your right to say no, and set limits without being hurt.

- Review your rules, and reconfirm the ones you've decided are important to enforce. Tell your child, when he is calm, that you will be doing that and that he must follow them if he is to continue living in your house. Investigate counseling and foster care.

- See a counselor, and get some help with your fear and the lack of structure in your house.

(See also questions 104, 132, and "Where to Go for Additional Support.")

Thanks to Carole Gesme,
Suggestion Circle from Minneapolis, Minnesota

175. How do we tell our teenagers that we are getting a divorce?

- Have a family meeting with everyone there. Make sure both parents take part in telling the children.

- Agree ahead of time that you will not put each other down in front of the children.

- When you tell them, be sure and talk about what will happen to them: where they will live and how each of you will continue to parent.

- Be available to the children after you tell them of your decision so they can come and talk.

- Take your time. You don't have to tell all the reasons when first talking about the divorce.

- Go to a family counselor with your family to get support during this time.

- Both of you say, "I love you, and even though your [mother/father] and I have decided to divorce, we will both be your parents and care for you. It is not your fault."

- Ask your spiritual leader for advice, support, and help during this time.

- Read the Duncans' *You're Divorced, But Your Children Aren't* or Jewett's *Helping Children Cope with Separation and Loss*. (See "Resources.")

(See also "Where to Go for Additional Support.")

Thanks to Gail Nordeman,
Suggestion Circle from Cincinnati, Ohio

176. This is my third marriage, and there are children from each, all teenagers. When we are together, how do I deal with their accusations of "favoritism"?

- Let them take turns choosing how family time will be spent.

- Set up a schedule that will allow special time for each child.

- Tell them you are glad that each of them wants attention and that you will be glad when they find a way to let you know without accusations.

- When a child says, "You like him better!" you say, "I care about you. Is there something special you need from me today?"

- Suggest, "You each fill up a different part of my heart. Right now, my left auricle needs attention, and that is your part."

- Have teens separate wants from needs. They may "want" to be king of the hill; they "need" love, support, limits, and the space to separate.

- Say, "It's OK for you to compete in activities. You don't have to compete for my love."

- Give recognition for individual talents and achievements.

- If the accusation is true, admit it and change.

- Read *How to Win as a Stepfamily,* by the Vishers.

(See also question 125, "Ages and Stages," and "Affirmations for Growth—Identity, Sexuality, and Separation.")

Thanks to Linda Buranen,
Suggestion Circle from Minneapolis, Minnesota

177. My stepdaughter feels she must lie to her mother in order to stay her full visiting time with her dad. How do I teach her to be honest, while protecting her right to visit us?

- Identify this as a problem that the parents must solve, and get the child out of the middle.

- Tell her clearly why you worry about this.

- Protecting visitation rights is up to your husband and his daughter. You get out of the middle.

- Insist that your husband get his ex-wife to adhere to the terms of the contract about visiting rights.

- Occasionally, go away from the house for the whole time of the visitation. Leave it to them.

- Be consistently honest yourself so the child can see the advantages.

- Her natural parents should work out this issue with attorneys or a counselor.

- Allow your stepchild to handle the situation as she sees she must, and discuss honesty versus expediency.

- Make sure the adults do the communicating about visitation so that the child doesn't have to lie.

- Offer love and stay out.

(See also "Affirmations for Growth—Identity, Sexuality, and Separation.")

Thanks to Sara Monser,
Suggestion Circle from Concord, California

178. I am a single parent. I work full time and travel some. How can I be a full-time parent to my fifteen-year-old son?

- Make a big calendar with your schedule and his. Then compare schedules once a week, and make dates for special time together.

- Talk with your son about how the two of you can work together to solve the problem.

- Arrange a car pool for getting him to his activities. Find other parents who will help out.

- Use a tape recorder for messages to each other.

- Find some substitute parents for him while you are gone.

- Find people he can phone for support and structure while you are gone.

- Call Big Brothers, Kinship, or other organizations that match boys with caring adult men.

- Set an hour aside each week just for talking about how each of your lives is going.

- Include him as much as you can in the planning and arranging of his life.

- Ask his grandparents to help.

- Call home often.

(See also "Ages and Stages" and "Parents of Teenagers Get Another Chance—Recycling.")

Thanks to Linda Buranen,
Suggestion Circle from Edina, Minnesota

Appendixes

Developmental Affirmations for All Ages

Being
(Stage I)

- I'm glad you are alive.
- You belong here.
- What you need is important to me.
- I'm glad you are you.
- You can grow at your own pace.
- You can feel all of your feelings.
- I love you and I care for you willingly.

Exploring and Doing
(Stage II)

- You can explore and experiment, and I will support and protect you.
- You can use all of your senses when you explore.
- You can do things as many times as you need to.
- You can know what you know.
- You can be interested in everything.
- I like to watch you initiate and grow and learn.
- I love you when you are active and when you are quiet.

The reader is encouraged to photocopy and post pages 210–213.

Thinking
(Stage III)

- I'm glad you are starting to think for yourself.
- It's OK for you to be angry, and I won't let you hurt yourself or others.
- You can say no and push and test limits as much as you need to.
- You can learn to think for yourself, and I will think for myself.
- You can think and feel at the same time.
- You can know what you need and ask for help.
- You can become separate from me, and I will continue to love you.

Identity and Power
(Stage IV)

- You can explore who you are and find out who other people are.
- You can be powerful and ask for help at the same time.
- You can try out different roles and ways of being powerful.
- You can find out the results of your behavior.
- All of your feelings are OK with me.
- You can learn what is pretend and what is real.
- I love who you are.

Structure
(Stage V)

- You can think before you say yes or no and learn from your mistakes.

- You can trust your intuition to help you decide what to do.

- You can find a way of doing things that works for you.

- You can learn the rules that help you live with others.

- You can learn when and how to disagree.

- You can think for yourself and get help instead of staying in distress.

- I love you even when we differ; I love growing with you.

Identity, Sexuality, and Separation
(Stage VI)

- You can know who you are and learn and practice skills for independence.

- You can learn the difference between sex and nurturing and be responsible for your needs and behavior.

- You can develop your own interests, relationships, and causes.

- You can learn to use old skills in new ways.

- You can grow in your maleness or femaleness and still be dependent at times.

- I look forward to knowing you as an adult.

- My love is always with you. I trust you to ask for my support.

Interdependence
(Stage VII)

- Your needs are important.

- You can be uniquely yourself and honor the uniqueness of others.

- You can be independent and interdependent.

- Through the years, you can expand your commitments to your own growth, to your family, your friends, your community, and to all humankind.

- You can build and examine your commitments to your values and causes, your roles and your tasks.

- You can be responsible for your contributions to each of your commitments.

- You can be creative, competent, productive, and joyful.

- You can trust your inner wisdom.

- You can say your hellos and good-byes to people, roles, dreams, and decisions.

- You can finish each part of your journey and look forward to the next.

- Your love matures and expands.

- You are lovable at every age.

The affirmations for stages I—VI are printed on ovals elsewhere in *Help! For Parents of Children frm Birth to Five* and in this volume. The affirmations for adults appear on ovals on the following page.

Interdependence
—For adults—

You can be creative, competent, productive and joyful.

You can trust your inner wisdom.

You can say your hellos and goodbyes to people, roles, dreams and decisions.

You can finish each part of your journey and look forward to the next.

Your love matures and expands.

You are lovable at every age.

Your needs are important.

You can be uniquely yourself and honor the uniqueness of others.

You can be independent and interdependent.

Through the years you can expand your commitments to your own growth, to your family, your friends, your community and to all humankind.

You can build and examine your commitments to your values and causes, your roles and your tasks.

You can be responsible for your contributions to each of your commitments.

**Copy these affirmation ovals for adults
and color them lilac or purple.
Post them for daily reading.**

Signs of Abuse and Neglect

Child abuse and neglect are prevalent—perhaps epidemic—in our society today. We editors feel strongly that all children are to be valued and cherished. We believe that children will be better protected when parents know the signs of child abuse.

Signs of abuse can vary with the age of the child. Listed here are signs that should arouse a parent's suspicions. If you find yourself worried or concerned about an abusive relationship between your child and another adult or older child, check it out.

Physical and behavioral signs that may indicate neglect or abuse include:

- Any unusual marks, particularly around the upper thighs, genitalia, or anus

- A sudden reluctance to wear shorts or bathing suits, which may mean revealing unusual marks around upper thighs

- Straight-line bruises that may come from a ruler or belt

- Hickey marks (purplish marks caused by sucking) on the neck

- Any statement by the child that he has been inappropriately touched

- Questioning by the child about how adults touch children, especially if the child will not state why he is asking the question

- Behavior problems, such as drug abuse, soiling, stealing, starting fires, or eating disorders

- Significant changes in school performance, attitudes, relationships, or truancy

- Signs of depression, such as subtle changes in response, drop in energy level, increased secretiveness or more time spent alone, increased difficulty in functioning

- Suicide gestures, such as notes saying, "I want to die," or attempts to overdose

- Any form of self-mutilation, including satanic symbols on the skin.

If you suspect abuse of any kind, find a way to protect your child. Get help if you need it. Report the abuser to the child protection service in your area. (See the "Common Pitfalls" sections and "Where to Go for Additional Support.")

Christine Ternand, M.D.

Safer Sex

Acquired immune deficiency syndrome (AIDS) kills! It is contracted through:

- Oral sex
- Vaginal sex
- Anal sex
- Shared dirty needles
- Contaminated blood transfusion
- Blood or sexual fluids exchanged through a break in the skin
- Being born to a mother who has AIDS

AIDS is epidemic and close to everyone. You may not have symptoms for a long time (sometimes years) after you contract this virus (HIV). There have been more people infected with HIV in the United States alone than the number of people who died in the Korean and Vietnam wars.

There is no safe sex. Strict abstinence from all of the ways listed here of contracting AIDS is the only sure preventative. Using a condom with spermicide conscientiously and without fail *reduces* the risk but does *not* eliminate it. Lesbians should call the AIDS hot line for advice about reducing risk with their specific practices. Sexual intercourse between two mutually un-infected faithful partners is only as preventative as the honesty of both partners.

If when you discuss safe sex, your children accuse you of being prudish, tell them that you care about their safety and that you have to tell them since this is what it takes to be safe. Wanting your kid to live is not prudish. *AIDS kills, and there is no cure.*

Tell them "If you choose to have sex, remember to be tested for the HIV virus at least twice (six months apart) before entering the sexual relationship; then remain mutually exclusive."

Dr. Everett Koop, the former surgeon general of the United States, implores us with this message, "My wish for you is to abstain from sex until you are grown, and find someone you really love and want as a lifetime companion. This keeps you both emotionally and physically safe and allows you to hold onto that gift that you can give only once and that helps you to create strong and lasting bonds with your partner. To marry and stay loyal allows you to give the gift of both love and life (no HIV risk)."

Samara Kemp, R.N.

How Is AIDS Spread Sexually?

HIV is transmitted through human secretions including semen and blood. If semen or blood comes in contact with a body surface that is easy for the virus to penetrate, HIV can be transmitted. Mucous membranes, such as those in the mouth, the vagina, and the interior of the anus, are all good avenues through which the virus can enter the bloodstream. Therefore, one can get the HIV virus from semen in the mouth (oral sex), anus (anal sex), or vagina (vaginal sex). A drop of semen contains enough of the virus to transmit HIV. Transmission of the virus from infected females may be higher during menstruation. Even condoms with spermicide (which attenuate some viruses) are not "perfect" protection. Anything less than a condom and spermicide is fooling oneself. Nothing else, including Saran Wrap or rubber dams, has been shown to be at all effective.

Christine Ternand, M.D.

Condom Use

This information is important for parents to discuss with their teens, preferably before teens become sexually active. *Postgraduate Medicine* reports that in 1991, on a nationwide average, 56 percent of teens (male and female) between the ages of thirteen and nineteen were sexually active. Forty percent of those teens had four or more partners within a year.

What to Use

- Every sexually active teen should carry spermicidal foam and condoms on a date. No sex without spermicidal foam and condom.

- Condoms alone or spermicide alone are only partially reliable in decreasing the risk of AIDS and pregnancy. Given the lifetime consequences of pregnancy or AIDS, even a small risk is too much.

- Condoms and foam used together are essential for reducing the risk of transmission of HIV, the virus which leads to AIDS. (See the first section under "Safe Sex?")

- Be sure the foam has the active ingredient nonoxynol-9, which is spermicidal and helps destroy the HIV virus.

- The combination of spermicidal foam and a condom is better than condoms alone.

- Buy only condoms lubricated with nonoxynol-9.
- Use condom and foam at each and every instance of sexual intercourse.

How to Use

- Read the instructions for the condoms in daylight.
- Make use of condom and foam as part of foreplay. If you use additional lubricant, don't use any oil-based lubricant such as Vaseline. It weakens the condom. K-Y jelly is water based and is acceptable.
- Put foam in no sooner than ten to fifteen minutes before intercourse.
- One drop of K-Y jelly may be used to lubricate the penis. Put the drop inside the tip of the condom before it is rolled into place.
- Put the condom on the erect penis before *any* sexual contact—oral, vaginal, or anal.
- Pull the condom on in such a way as to leave space at the tip of the condom for semen to collect.
- Withdraw immediately after the male has an orgasm. A flaccid penis causes the condom to leak.
- Grab the condom tightly at the base of the penis after the male has an orgasm in order to get the penis out with the condom in place.

Caution

- Do *not* reuse a condom!
- Remember that even careful condom use is no guarantee of safety. Sexual intercourse with one uninfected mutually faithful partner is the only "safe sex."

- Also remember, if you choose to have sex, to be tested for the HIV virus at least twice (six months apart) before entering the relationship; then remain mutually exclusive.

Samara Kemp, R.N., and Beth Aversa, R.N.

The Fuss Box

A fuss box is a place to vent your anger so you can think clearly about what to do in order to help yourself or others.

The purpose of the fuss box is to help people

- Claim their anger
- Claim their right to express anger
- Claim responsibility for their anger
- Have a way to express anger without hurting themselves or other people and without other people interfering with the expression of the anger or trying to "fix" it
- Have a way to clear out the anger and get on with solutions to the problem.

How do you make a fuss box? Find a sturdy box or carton big enough to stand in and still have a bit of space in which to move around. Write "FUSS BOX" in bold letters on all sides of the box so that anyone entering the room while you are fussing will be reminded that you are to be left alone because you are in the fuss box.

How do you use the fuss box? First, let everyone in your family group (or wherever you use the box) know the purpose of the box and the rules for using it. Write the rules on a poster that you bring out whenever you use the box.

Fuss Box Rules

1) Choose the place with care.

2) Stay in the box while fussing.

3) Say whatever you want to.

4) Other people do not interfere.

5) Fuss until you feel your energy switch.

6) Then step out of the box and decide how to make the situation better.

These Rules Are Important

1) Select with care the place where you will use the box. Use it only in a place where people care about you. Do not use it in front of young children who may not understand what you are doing or who might be frightened. Don't use it in front of people who might use what you say in the box to "get you" later.

2) Stand in the box while you are fussing.

3) Say anything you want to. Your words may be unreasonable, unwarranted, or unfair. Express your frustrations.

4) Other people are to stay out of your anger. They can sympathize, but they are not to argue or try to fix or console you. They must leave the room if they are tempted to feel any hurt, fear, or responsibility for your feelings.

5) Fuss as vigorously as you want until you feel your energy switch; this usually takes from about thirty seconds to four or five minutes. When you start to feel calm or chuckle at yourself, say, "I feel better now," and step outside the box.

6) Stand beside the fuss box, and decide at least one thing you will do to make the situation better. Do it.

CAUTION: Do not step outside the box and continue to fuss. If you do that, get back into the box and do your fussing there. Otherwise, you will encourage yourself to continue fussing instead of solving problems.

CAUTION: Use a real box. People who do not use a real box are not setting clear boundaries.

CAUTION: Do not use the fuss box just to vent anger or frustration and then do nothing about the situation. That would be using the box to *encourage* your frustration and to make life worse instead of better. Also, use the fuss box for ordinary frustrations. Get help from a counselor if you have deep rage.

The fuss box can be used with six- to twelve-year-old children. Insist that they and you follow the rules whenever the fuss box is used.

Jean Illsley Clarke

Time-Out

What Is Time-Out?

Time-out is a technique used to interrupt unacceptable behavior for a few minutes by removing the child from the "scene of the action." Time-out is a calming device, not a punishment.

When and Where to Use It

Use a time-out for stopping inappropriate behavior before it reaches oppressive or assaultive proportions or for serious violations of your family's rules. Put the child in a safe, boring place within your view.

The time-out should be short enough so that the child has a chance to go back to the original situation after the time-out is over and learn acceptable behavior. One minute or less for each year of the child's age is usually appropriate.

Procedure

Before using a time-out, see if your child understands the concepts of "think" and "quiet."

The first few times, do this:

1) Explain a time-out to the child.

2) Explain when it will be used.

3) Walk the child through the steps.

4) Time the quiet time only (not the whining, crying, or fussing).

5) Tell the child the time-out is over when the time is up or when he tells you he has decided how to change his behavior.

6) Return the child to the situation, and reinforce appropriate behavior.

This summary of the time-out strategy is from Elizabeth Crary's *Without Spanking or Spoiling*. (See "Resources.") See her book for a more complete description of the uses of and pitfalls of using time-outs.

The Editors

Four Ways Young People Separate

One of the tasks of adolescents is to separate from parents in preparation for becoming independent.

Some teens separate pleasantly or with excitement and anticipation. Others act angry, as if the people they are separating from are despicable, disgusting, or at least terribly boring. The following paragraphs describe four ways in which young people carry out the task of separating.

- The first way of separating is to *leave.* Here the teen leaves home in either a calm or angry way, is gone for some time, and then comes home and functions as a responsible adult in the extended family. She may then live at home or someplace else.

- The second way of separating is to *go out and back.* This child leaves home for a while, then is back home, then lives with friends for a few months, then moves home again. She repeats this process several times. Each time she comes home she is more self-sufficient and more responsible. The process of separation is completed when the young person is living at home or someplace else and is functioning as an equal adult in the world, not as a financially or emotionally dependent child.

- The third way of separating is to *stay at home.* The teen remains at home and becomes a financially responsible, emotionally differentiated adult.

- To be *ejected* by the family is the fourth way of separating. The child who chooses this way uses family energy to help her move. She does whatever it takes to get the family to say firmly, "Sorry, you can't live here and do that." The child leaves, and the separation is complete when the child has become a full, responsible adult in the community and in the extended family system. This way is not to be confused with "kicking a child out" with threats and criticism that leave deep scars on both parents and adolescents.

Any of these four ways can result in successful separations. Sometimes parents and teens experience unnecessary stress when teens choose to separate in a way that is different from the one parents expect or the one they used themselves.

Jean Illsley Clarke

How to Lead a Suggestion Circle

The person leading the circle will do the following:

1) Ask the participants to sit in a circle.

2) Ask a member of the group to write down the suggestions for the person asking for help.

3) Ask the participants to respond to the question with their best suggestion; stop them if they ramble.

4) Go around the circle in order.

5) Ask people *not* to comment on each other's responses, and interrupt them if they do.

6) Offer people the right to pass without being challenged.

The person asking for a Suggestion Circle will do this:

1) State the problem in a clear, short statement.

2) Respond to each member's suggestion with a "thank you."

3) Go home, think, and act.

Each group member will either respond with one short, quality answer or will pass. A group of twelve people can respond to a problem in about five minutes.

Harold Nordeman

Telephone Circle

A Suggestion Circle can also be done by telephone.

1) When you have a problem that you need help with, phone six friends.

2) Clearly and quickly explain the problem to each friend, and ask for his or her best suggestion. Writing the problem out before you call may help you state it more clearly.

3) Listen to the suggestion and write it down.

4) Do not comment on the suggestion, other than to say, "Thank you."

5) After you have phoned each friend, look over your list of suggestions and decide which to use. Acknowledge the support that you have received from your friends.

Sandra Sittko

Leader's Checklist for Clean, Clear Leadership of a Suggestion Circle

___I explained clearly to the people in the group how a Suggestion Circle works. (I may have decided to run one for myself first with a new group.)

___I posted the Suggestion Circle poster.

___I helped the focus person to clarify his or her situation so that the focus person, the group, and I all held a common understanding of the problem.

___I made a contract with the focus person to listen to all the suggestions offered and to say only "Thank you," and I supported the focus person in keeping that contract.

___I made clear that the "thank you" was for the person's willingness to give a suggestion and was not a comment on the quality of the suggestion.

___I reminded the group to offer their best (high-quality) ideas, one at a time, in a concise sentence or two, and I praised them for doing that.

___I reminded myself and the group of the ground rules, particularly the right to pass, and enforced them as needed.

___I offered the opportunity to have someone in the group write down the suggestions for the focus person.

___I returned to group members who passed the first time around in case they wished to offer a suggestion later.

___I invited the focus person to consider the suggestions and to use them in ways that fit for him or her; I also invited the focus person to report back to the group but emphasized that there was no pressure to do so.

___I ran the Suggestion Circle in three to ten minutes, depending on the size of the group.

___If there were more than twenty people, I divided them into groups of ten to fifteen and got others to help lead so we could run simultaneous circles.

Deane Gradous

Suggestion Circle

- One problem,
  one sentence

> Think
> One best suggestion,
>   one sentence
> Write

- Thank you
- Think, choose and use

Where to Go for Additional Support

If you have talked with your family and friends, tried the ideas offered by the Suggestion Circles in this book, and still feel stuck with a problem, here are some places to call for additional help or for parenting classes. If you have difficulty finding a telephone number after looking in both the white and the yellow pages, call any of these sources and ask them to help you find the number you need.

Community Services

Crisis or hot-line numbers

YMCA, YWCA, or a local church or synagogue

Chemical abuse treatment centers

Chemical abuse prevention programs

Parents Without Partners International

Community civic centers

Women's or men's support groups

Battered women's and children's shelters

Big Brothers/Big Sisters

Local hospitals

Alcoholics Anonymous

Parents Anonymous

Alateen

Al-Anon

Mothers Against Drunk Driving (MADD)

Students Against Drunk Driving (SADD)

National Child Abuse Hot Line: 1-800-4-A-CHILD

Schools

Community education (run by the local school district)

Colleges or universities

Community colleges

Vocational and technical schools

Government

Community mental health center or clinic

Public health nurse or department

Child protection services

Family service agencies

County social service agencies

About AIDS: 1-800-342-AIDS

Private Services

Psychologists, social workers, psychiatrists, therapists, family counselors

Interview the persons who will help you to see if they know about the area in which you need support. If you don't get the help you need, go somewhere else until you do.

The Editors

Resources

Ages and Stages

Ames, Louise Bates, and Haber, Carol Chase. *Your Eight-Year-Old.* New York: Delacorte Press, 1989.

Ames, Louise Bates, Ilg, Frances, and Baker, Sidney. *Your Ten-to Fourteen-Year-Old.* New York: Delta, 1988.

Calladine, Carole. *One Terrific Year.* New York: Harper & Row, 1985.

Clarke, Jean Illsley. *The Terrific Twos.* Plymouth, MN: Daisy Tapes, 1983. (Write to: Daisy Press, 16535 9th Avenue N, Plymouth, MN 55447.)

––––––. *The Wonderful Busy Ones.* Plymouth, MN: Daisy Tapes, 1983. (Write to: Daisy Press, 16535 9th Avenue N, Plymouth, MN 55447.)

Elkind, David. *All Grown Up and No Place to Go.* Reading, MA: Addison-Wesley, 1984.

––––––. *The Hurried Child: Growing Up Too Fast, Too Soon.* Reading, MA: Addison-Wesley, 1989.

Levin, Pamela. *Becoming the Way We Are.* Deerfield Beach, FL: Health Communications, 1988.

Piaget, Jean. *The Child and Reality.* New York: Grossman Publishers, 1973.

––––––. *Conception of Reality in the Child.* New York: Ballantine, 1986.

Self-Esteem

Anderson, Eugene, Redman, George, and Rogers, Charlotte. *Self-Esteem for Tots to Teens*. Wayzata, MN: Parenting and Teaching Publications, 1991.

Bean, Reynold, et al. *How to Raise Teenagers' Self-Esteem*. San Jose, CA: Enrich Division/OHAUS, 1983.

Clarke, Jean Illsley. *Self-Esteem: A Family Affair*. New York: Harper & Row, 1985.

Clarke, Jean Illsley, and Gesme, Carole. *Affirmation Ovals: One Hundred Thirty-nine Ways to Give and Get Affirmations*. Plymouth, MN: Daisy Press, 1988. (Write to: Daisy Press, 16535 9th Avenue N, Plymouth, MN 55447.)

Kaufman, Gershen. *Shame: The Power of Caring*. Cambridge, MA: Shenkman, 1985.

Kaufman, Gershen, and Raphael, Lev. *Stick Up for Yourself*. Minneapolis, MN: Free Spirit Publishing, 1990.

Levenkron, Steven. *The Best Little Girl in the World*. Chicago: Warner Books, 1989.

Steiner, Claude. *Warm Fuzzy Tale*. Rolling Hills Estate, CA: Jalmar Press, 1977.

Values

Baldwin, Bruce A. *Beyond the Cornucopia Kids*. Wilmington, NC: Direction Dynamics, 1988.

Glenn, Stephen H., and Nelsen, Jane. *Raising Self-Reliant Children in a Self-Indulgent World*. Rocklin, CA: Prima Publishing and Communications, 1988.

Williams, Lynne H., and Berman, Henry S. *The Too-Precious Child*. New York: Warner Books, 1987.

Skill Building

Greenberger, Ellen, and Steinberg, Laurence. *When Teenagers Work.* New York: Basic Books, 1988.

Snyder, Chris. *Teaching Your Child About Money.* Reading, MA: Addison-Wesley, 1984.

Health

Bell, Ruth. *Changing Bodies, Changing Lives.* New York: Random House, 1988.

Boston Women's Health Book Collective. *The New Our Bodies, Ourselves.* New York: Simon & Schuster, 1985.

Heegaard, Marjorie, and Ternand, Christine. *When a Family Gets Diabetes.* Minneapolis, MN: Chronimed Publishing, 1990.

Hynes, Angela. *Puberty: An Illustrated Manual for Parents and Daughters.* New York: TOR, RGA Publishing Group, 1989.

Levenkron, Steven. *The Best Little Girl in the World.* Chicago: Warner Books, 1989.

Madaras, Lynda, and Madaras, Area. *What's Happening to My Body? Book for Girls.* New York: Newmarket Press, 1988.

Madaras, Lynda, and Saavedra, Dane. *What's Happening to My Body? Book for Boys.* New York: Newmarket Press, 1988.

Mayle, Peter. *What's Happening to Me?* Secaucus, NJ: Carol Publishing Group, 1975.

McCoy, Kathy, and Wibbelsman, Charles. *The New Teenage Body Book.* Los Angeles: Body Press/Price Stern Sloan, 1987.

Rathers, Spenser, and Boughn, Susan. *AIDS: What Every Student Should Know.* Fort Worth, TX: Harcourt Brace, 1993.

Rosenberg, Ellen. *Growing Up Feeling Good.* New York: Beaufort Books, 1983.

Drugs

Black, Claudia. *It Will Never Happen to Me!* Colorado Springs, CO: M.A.C. Printing and Publications Division, 1982.

Braun, Ken. *When Saying No Isn't Enough: How to Keep the Children You Love Off Drugs*. New York: New American Library/Penguin, 1988.

Cretcher, Dorothy. *Steering Clear: Helping Your Child Through the High-Risk Drug Years*. New York: Harper & Row, 1982.

Donlan, Joan. *I Never Saw the Sun Rise*. Minneapolis, MN: CompCare Publications, 1977.

DuPont, Robert J., Jr. *Getting Tough on Gateway Drugs: A Guide for the Family*. Washington, DC: American Psychiatric Press, 1984.

Engel, Joel. *Addicted in Their Own Words: Kids Talking About Drugs*. New York: Tom Doherty Associates Book by RGA Publishing Group, 1989.

Hodgson, Harriett W. *A Parent's Survival Guide: How to Cope When Your Kid Is Using Drugs*. Cambridge, MA: Harper/Hazelden, 1986.

Otteson, Orlo, and Townsend, John. *Kids and Drugs: A Parent's Guide*. New York: CFF Publishing, 1983.

Polson, Beth, and Newton, Miller. *Not My Kid: A Parent's Guide to Kids and Drugs*. New York: Avon, 1985.

Typpo, Marion H., and Hastings, Jill M. *An Elephant in the Living Room*. Minneapolis, MN: CompCare Publications, 1984.

Van Ost, William C., M.D., and Van Ost, Elaine. *Warning Signs: In-Time Intervention in Drug and Alcohol Abuse*. New York: Warner Books, 1988.

Yoveha, Geraldine, and Seixas, Judith S. *Drugs, Alcohol, and Your Children*. New York: Crown Publishers, 1989.

Sex

Calderone, Mary S., and Johnson, Eric W. *The Family Book About Sexuality*. New York: HarperCollins, 1990.

Comfort, Alex, and Comfort, Jane. *The Facts of Love: Living, Loving, and Growing Up*. New York: Ballantine, 1980.

Gayle, Jay, Ph.D. *A Parent's Guide to Teenage Sexuality*. New York: Henry Holt, 1989.

———. *A Young Man's Guide to Sex*. Los Angeles: Price Stern, 1988.

———. *A Young Woman's Guide to Sex*. Los Angeles: Price Stern, 1988.

Gordon, Sol. *Why Love Is Not Enough*. Boston: Bob Adams Publishers, 1988.

Silverstein, Herma. *Teenage and Pregnant*. Englewood Cliffs, NJ: Julian Messner, 1988.

Safety

Adams, Caren, Fay, Jennifer, and Loreen-Martin, Jan. *NO Is Not Enough*. San Luis Obispo, CA: Impact Publishers, 1984.

Hagans, Kathryn B., and Case, Joyce. *When Your Child Has Been Molested*. Lexington, MA: Lexington Books, 1988.

Leder, Jane Mersky. *Dead Serious: A Book for Teenagers About Teenage Suicide*. New York: Avon, 1987.

McEvoy, Alan W., and Brookings, Jeff B. *If She Is Raped*. Holmes Beach, FL: Learning Publications, 1984.

Newman, Susan. *Never Say Yes to a Stranger*. New York: Perigee Books, 1985.

———. *It Won't Happen to Me: True Stories of Teen Alcohol and Drug Abuse*. New York: Perigee Books, 1987.

Food

Satter, Ellyn. *How to Get Your Kid to Eat But Not Too Much*. Palo Alto, CA: Bull Publishing, 1987.

Stoltz, Sandra Gordon. *The Food Fix*. Englewood Cliffs, NJ: Prentice Hall, 1983.

Relationships

With Others

Adams, Caren, and Fay, Jennifer. *No More Secrets*. San Luis Obispo, CA: Impact Publishers, 1981.

Ames, Louise Bates, et al. *He Hit Me First*. New York: Dembner Books, 1981.

Banks, Ann, and Evans, Nancy. *Goodbye, House: A Kid's Guide to Moving*. New York: Harmony Books, 1980.

Bozarth-Campbell, Alla. *Life Is Goodbye—Life Is Hello: Grieving Through All Kinds of Loss*. Minneapolis, MN: CompCare, 1982.

Bradley, Buff. *Where Do I Belong? A Kids' Guide to Stepfamilies*. Reading, MA: Addison-Wesley, 1982.

Brown, Margaret. *The Dead Bird*. Reading, MA: Addison-Wesley, 1958.

Clarke, Jean Illsley. *Ouch, That Hurts! A Handbook for People Who Hate Criticism*. Plymouth, MN: Daisy Press, 1983. (Write to: Daisy Press, 16535 9th Avenue N, Plymouth, MN 55447.)

Clubb, Angela Neumann. *Love in the Blended Family*. Toronto: Family Books/NC Press, 1988.

Davis, Diane. *Something Is Wrong at My House*. Seattle, WA: Parenting Press, 1985.

Dreikurs, Rudolf, Gould, Shirley, and Corsini, Raymond J. *Family Council: The Dreikurs Technique for Putting an End to War Between Parents and Children (and Between Children and Children)*. Chicago: Henry Regnery, 1974.

Duncan, T. Roger, and Duncan, Darlene. *You're Divorced, But Your Children Aren't*. Englewood Cliffs, NJ: Prentice Hall, 1979.

Einstein, Elizabeth, and Albert, Linda. *Strengthening Your Stepfamily*. Circle Pines, MN: American Guidance Service, 1986.

Ekman, Paul. *Why Kids Lie*. New York: Penguin Books, 1989.

Fahlberg, Vera. *Attachment and Separation*. Michigan Department of Social Sciences, 1979.

Fassler, Joan. *My Grandpa Died Today*. New York: Human Sciences Press, 1983.

Fleming, Don, Ph.D. *How to Stop the Battle with Your Teenager*. Englewood Cliffs, NJ: Prentice Hall, 1989.

Gesme, Carole. *Paper People*. 1989. (Write to: Carole Gesme, 4036 Kerry Court, Minnetonka, MN 55345.)

Gesme, Carole, and Peterson, Larry. *Help for Kids! Understanding Your Feelings About Moving*. Minneapolis, MN: Pinetree Press, 1991. (Write to: Pinetree Press, 4036 Kerry Court, Minnetonka, MN 55345.)

Getzoff, Ann, and McClenahan, Carolyn. *Stepkids: A Survival Guide for Teenagers in Stepfamilies . . . and for Stepparents Doubtful of Their Own Survival*. New York: Warner Books, 1984.

Grollman, Earl A. *Talking About Death*. Boston: Beacon Press, 1976.

Heegaard, Marge E. *Coping with Death and Grief*. Minneapolis, MN: Lerner Publications, 1990.

Jeffers, Susan. *Feel the Fear, and Do It Anyway*. San Diego, CA: Harcourt Brace Jovanovich, 1987.

Jewett, Claudia L. *Helping Children Cope with Separation and Loss*. Cambridge, MA: Harvard Common Press, 1982.

Johnston-Patlps, Ethel. *Tatterhood and Other Tales*. New York: Feminist Press, 1978.

Lewis-Steere, Cynthia. *Stepping Lightly.* Minneapolis, MN: CompCare Publications, 1981.

Lifton, Betty Jean. *Lost and Found: The Adoption Experience.* New York: Perennial Library, 1988.

Rofes, Eric. *The Kids' Book of Divorce by, for, and About Kids.* New York: Random House, 1982.

Sanford, Linda. *Silent Children: A Parents Guide to the Prevention of Child Abuse.* New York: McGraw-Hill, 1982.

Visher, John, and Visher, Emily. *How to Win as a Stepfamily.* Chicago: Contemporary Books, 1982.

Wachter, Oralee. *No More Secrets for Me.* Boston: Little, Brown, 1983.

With the Environment/World

Earthworks Group. *Fifty Simple Things Kids Can Do to Save the Earth.* Kansas City, MO: Andrews and McNeel, 1990.

Gesme, Carole. *Help for Kids: Understanding Your Feelings About the War.* Plymouth, MN: Pinetree Press, 1985. (Write to: Pinetree Press, 4036 Kerry Court, Minnetonka, MN 55345.)

May, Rollo. *Power and Innocence: A Search for the Sources of Violence.* New York: W. W. Norton, 1972.

Seymour, John, and Girardet, Herbert. *Blueprint for a Green Planet: Your Practical Guide to Restoring the World's Environment.* Englewood Cliffs, NJ: Prentice Hall, 1987.

Sweeney, Duane. *The Peace Catalogue: A Guidebook to a Positive Future.* Seattle, WA: Press for Peace, 1984.

Rules and Discipline

Bayard, Robert T., and Bayard, Jean. *How to Deal with Your Acting-Up Teenager.* New York: Evans, 1983.

Bodenhamer, Gregory. *Back in Control: How to Get Your Children to Behave.* Englewood Cliffs, NJ: Prentice Hall, 1983.

Bosch, Carl. *Bully on the Bus. The Decision Is Yours* series. Seattle, WA: Parenting Press, 1989.

———. *Making the Grade. The Decision Is Yours* series. Seattle, WA: Parenting Press, 1991.

Crary, Elizabeth. *Finders Keepers. The Decision Is Yours* series. Seattle, WA: Parenting Press, 1987.

———. *Kids Can Cooperate.* Seattle, WA: Parenting Press, 1984.

———. *Without Spanking or Spoiling.* Second Edition. Seattle, WA: Parenting Press, 1993.

Eyre, Linda, and Eyre, Richard. *Teaching Children Responsibility.* New York: Ballantine, 1986.

Little, Bill. *This Will Drive You Sane.* Minneapolis, MN: CompCare Publications, 1980.

Meeks, Carolyn Ann. *Prescriptions for Parenting.* New York: Warner Books, 1990.

Nelson, Jane. *Positive Discipline.* Fair Oaks, CA: Sunrise Press, 1985.

Windell, James. *Discipline: A Sourcebook of Fifty Fail-Safe Techniques for Parents.* New York: Macmillan, 1991.

Wyckoff, Jerry, and Unell, Barbara. *How to Discipline Your Six-to Twelve-Year-Old Without Losing Your Mind.* New York: Doubleday, 1991.

York, Phyllis, and York, David. *Toughlove Solutions.* New York: Bantam Books, 1985.

Future

Jobs

Greenberger, Ellen, and Steinberg, Laurence. *When Teenagers Work.* New York: Basic Books, 1988.

Snyder, Chris. *Teaching Your Child About Money.* Reading, MA: Addison-Wesley, 1984.

Leaving Home

Banks, Ann, and Evans, Nancy. *Goodbye, House: A Kid's Guide to Moving*. New York: Harmony Books, 1980.

Bradshaw, John. *Homecoming*. New York: Bantam Books, 1990.

Parenting

Barty, Wayne R., and Rosor, R. A. *Surviving with Kids*. San Luis Obispo, CA: Impact Publishers, 1983.

Bell, Ruth, and Zeiger, Leni. *Talking with Your Teenager: A Book for Parents*. New York: Random House, 1983.

Bettelheim, Bruno. *A Good Enough Parent*. New York: Knopf, 1987.

Budd, Linda. *Living with the Active Alert Child*. Englewood Cliffs, NJ: Prentice Hall, 1990.

Dads Only. (Monthly magazine). (Write to: P.O. Box 270616, San Diego, CA 92128.)

Dreikurs, Rudolf. *Children: The Challenge*. New York: Hawthorn-Dutton, 1987.

Dreikurs, Rudolf, Gould, Shirley, and Corsini, Raymond J. *Family Council: The Dreikurs Technique for Putting an End to War Between Parents and Children (and Between Children and Children)*. Chicago: Henry Regnery, 1974.

Elkind, David. *The Hurried Child: Growing Up Too Fast, Too Soon*. Reading, MA: Addison-Wesley, 1989.

Faber, Adele, and Mazlish, Elaine. *How to Talk So Kids Will Listen and Listen So Kids Will Talk*. New York: Avon, 1982.

———. *Siblings Without Rivalry*. New York: W. W. Norton, 1987.

Gordon, Thomas. *Parent Effectiveness Training*. New York: Peter H. Wyden, 1974.

Gould, Shirley. *Teenagers: The Continuing Challenge.* New York: Dutton, 1977.

Hayes, E. Kent. *Why Good Kids Have Bad Parents: How to Make Sure That Your Child Grows Up Right.* New York: Doubleday, 1989.

Herbert, Martin. *Living with Teenagers.* Oxford, England: Basil Blackwell, 1987.

Johnson, Spencer. *The One-Minute Father/Mother.* New York: William Morrow, 1983.

Kurcinka, Mary Sheedy. *Raising Your Spirited Child.* New York: HarperCollins, 1991.

Maidment, Robert. *Straight Talk: A Guide to Saying More with Less.* Gretna, LA: Pelican, 1983.

McBride, Angela Barron. *How to Enjoy a Good Life with Your Teenagers.* Tucson, AZ: Fisher Books, 1987.

Popkin, Michael. *Active Parenting.* New York: Harper & Row, 1987.

Powell, Douglas H. *Teenagers: When to Worry, What to Do.* New York: Doubleday, 1987.

Tuscherer, Pamela. *The New High-Tech Threat to Children.* Bend, OR: Pennington Publishing, 1988.

Vedral, Joyce L., Ph.D. *My Teenager Is Driving Me Crazy.* New York: Ballantine, 1989.

Weinhaus, Evonne, and Friedman, Karen. *Stop Struggling with Your Teen.* New York: Viking Penguin, 1988.

Parents

Ashery, Rebecca Sayer, and Basen, Michele Margolin. *The Parents-with-Careers Workbook.* Washington, DC: Acropolis Books, 1983.

Clarke, Jean Illsley, and Dawson, Connie. *Growing Up Again: Parenting Ourselves, Parenting Our Children.* New York: HarperCollins, 1989.

Hendricks, Gay, and Wills, Russel. *The Centering Book.* Englewood Cliffs, NJ: Prentice Hall, 1989.

Lerner, Harriet Goldhor. *The Dance of Anger.* New York: Harper & Row, 1985.

———. *The Dance of Intimacy.* New York: Harper & Row, 1989.

Activities/Games

Covert, James T., and Smith, Jan. *Memory Makers.* Portland, OR: Frank Amato Publications, 1988.

Gesme, Carole. *The Love Game.* 1988. (Write to: Carole Gesme, 4036 Kerry Court, Minnetonka, MN 55345.)

———. *Ups and Downs with Feelings.* Seven explorer games, ages six years through adult. 1985. (Write to: Carole Gesme, 4036 Kerry Court, Minnetonka, MN 55345.)

Heegaard, Marge E. *When Mom and Dad Separate.* Minneapolis, MN: Woodland Press, 1990.

———. *When Someone Very Special Dies.* Minneapolis, MN: Woodland Press, 1988.

Hoyle, Edmund. *Hoyle's Card Games.* Boston: Routledge & Kegan Paul, 1979.

Orlick, Terry. *Cooperative Sports and Games Book.* New York: Pantheon Books, 1978.

Zakich, Rhea. *The Ungame.* (A board game with cards and playing pieces). Anaheim, CA: Ungame Company, 1975.

Index

Other Learning Materials Available

Developmental Affirmation Ovals are laminated colored ovals that come in different sizes as bookmarks, punch-outs, or stickers. Each set includes all fifty-four affirmations.

Developmental Tapes, by Jean Illsley Clarke, are audiocassette tapes that present important information about children and the nurturing they need. Told in both male and female voices, they are useful tools for adults and for helping older children understand their little brothers' and sisters' needs and behavior. Each is twelve to eighteen minutes long.

The twelve *Ups and Downs with Feelings* starter games for ages three to six and the seven *Explorer* games for ages six to adult, by Carole Gesme, help children and adults recognize, name, and be responsible for their feelings.

The *Love Game,* by Carole Gesme, is an everybody-wins board game that lets people absorb unconditional love messages while they follow the directions indicated by the roll of the dice.

Also by Carol Gesme, the fast-paced *Capture a Feeling* card game, for ages six to one hundred and six, is a playful way for two to nine players to learn about handling feelings.

Feeling Faces Paper People, by Carole Gesme, includes over one hundred paper pieces to color and cut. Match the feeling faces to the vests and sweatshirts with messages for growth and health.

The *Sing Yes!* audiocassette, by Darrell Faires, contains sixty-three singable, easy-to-remember songs based on the affirmations. A sampler tape of fourteen songs is also available. Sung by both male and female vocalists.

WE: A Newsletter for People Who Care About Self-Esteem includes theories and activities about children and parenting and is edited by Jean Illsley Clarke.

For more information, including prices, write to:

Daisy Press
16535 9th Avenue N
Minneapolis, MN 55447

About the Editors

Jean Illsley Clarke, M.A., is the author of the book *Self-Esteem: A Family Affair*, coauthor of *Growing Up Again*, and author of parenting programs based on both of these books. The Suggestion Circle technique comes from those programs. She teaches people how to facilitate groups and has written *Who, Me Lead a Group?* She is a transactional analyst, a nationally certified parent educator, and a mother of three. She and her husband, Richard, live in Minnesota.

Deane Gradous, M.B.A., Ph.D., is mother to Allen and Susan, both graduate engineers. She is married to Fred, also an engineer. More than a decade after earning a business degree, Deane returned to the University of Minnesota to pursue her interest in improving human performance at work. She says that providing clear expectations, essential equipment, and skills training *before* asking people to perform a new task is much better than leaving them to their own devices and then telling them what they did wrong. In other words, she strongly believes in structuring for success.

Sara Monser, M.S., and her husband, Carl, have four young-adult children and are foster parents in a "fragile-infant program." Sara holds a master's degree in educational psychology. In addition to teaching development and family communication classes at Diablo Valley Community College in Pleasant Hill, California, she coordinates the foster care education program for the college.

Gail Nordeman, R.N., B.A., and Harold Nordeman have parented five teenagers and are the founders and directors of A Growing Place, an educational, counseling, and consulting center in Cincinnati, Ohio. They have taught preadolescent sex education classes and Self-Esteem: A Family Affair workshops, and have coauthored "Affirmations for Adult Children of Alcoholics." Gail is a registered nurse with a clinical provisional teaching membership in the International Transactional Analysis Association. Harold is a personal communication consultant and author of "The Suggestion Circle as a Therapeutic Tool."

Sandra Sittko earned her M.S.W. from the George Warren Brown School of Social Work, Washington University, Saint Louis, Missouri. She lives in Saint Paul, Minnesota, where she leads the "Self-Esteem: A Family Affair" parenting class and uses the skills with her clients, her family, and her friends. Sandra especially thanks her parents, Dr. William and Phyllis Sittko, for providing many opportunities for personal growth and high self-esteem.

As a pediatrician, Christine Ternand, M.D., sees ten to twenty families daily and learns with them about human growth and development and about parenting. She specializes in pediatric endocrinology. She uses parenting education in her practice at Group Health to help create a preventive rather than just problem-solving practice. She is the coauthor of *When a Family Gets Diabetes.* She and her husband Doug expand their parenting skills with their wonderful sons—Alex, Eric, and Kevin.